£ 12.99

DYSLEXIA
From a Cultural Perspec

ASHER & MARTIN HOYLES

H
HANSIB

Published by Hansib Publications in 2007

Hansib Publications Limited
P.O. Box 226, Hertford, Hertfordshire, SG14 3WY,
United Kingdom

Email: info@hansib-books.com
Website: www.hansib-books.com

A catalogue record of this book is
available from the British Library

ISBN 978-1-870518-89-5

Cover designed by Stefan Brazzo
Printed and bound by The Alden Press, Oxford, UK

"Gather together in our name."

ACKNOWLEDGEMENTS

We thank all those interviewed for the book and the following for their invaluable help: Arif Ali, Kash Ali and Isha Persaud at Hansib, Joan Dunbar-Pattrick and the children of Gospel Oak Primary School, Mike Juggins, Steven O'Brien, Abiola Ogunsola, Qona Rankin, Gavin Reid, Rosa for the jokes, Alan Seymour, Ken Townson for the photo of Donald Schloss, Keith Wynn for the photo of Asher.

THE AUTHORS: Asher Hoyles is an additional support tutor, specialising in dyslexia, at NewVIc Sixth Form College in Newham, east London. She is also a performance poet who runs performance poetry workshops.

Martin Hoyles taught in Newham secondary schools and at the University of East London. He has written books on gardening, childhood and literacy. His latest book is *The Axe Laid to the Root: The Story of Robert Wedderburn* (Hansib, 2004).

Together, Asher & Martin wrote *Remember Me: Achievements of Mixed Race People, Past & Present* (Hansib, 1999) and *Moving Voices: Black Performance Poetry* (Hansib, 2002).

CONTENTS

INTRODUCTION

"When I was permanently excluded from school, I was called a failure. I was only 13 and illiterate, but I had memorised the Bible, The Philosophy and Opinions of Marcus Garvey, the teachings of Malcolm X and much of the Koran. I could recite hundreds of traditional Jamaican songs and poems (as well as my own) ... Although I was unable to read, my exposure to the oral tradition seemed to expand my ability to memorise information."

Benjamin Zephaniah 'The Teacher' May 1999

■ ■ ■

"Simultaneous oppression, in this instance, refers to the fact that disabled Black people's realities are shaped by racist and disablist structures at the same time."

Ayesha Vernon 'Multiple Oppression and the Disabled People's Movement' 1998

■ ■ ■

Where are the Black dyslexics? If you look in the publications of most dyslexia organisations, you would be forgiven for thinking there aren't any! Yet dyslexia is no respecter of race. It occurs in all countries and cultures. It has a genetic base and runs in families. If both parents are dyslexic, the child has an 80% chance of being dyslexic.

The 1999 MacPherson report into the death of Stephen Lawrence concluded that every institution should examine its policies and outcomes to ensure that no section of the community is placed at a disadvantage. This should clearly include dyslexia. But if you are Black and dyslexic in our society, you are doubly disadvantaged. Add working-class and you have triple oppression! What unites these categories is that all three are often labelled 'stupid' and 'lazy'.

In a book entitled 'Constructions of Disability', published in 2004, Claire Tregaskis, herself a wheelchair user, made a study of a leisure centre. She asked one of the senior managers, who was Black, what were the similarities between Black people's and disabled people's experience. He replied: "Always having to fight for things that

What did the Dyslexic say to the Tobogganist?

"10 Silk Cut, please."

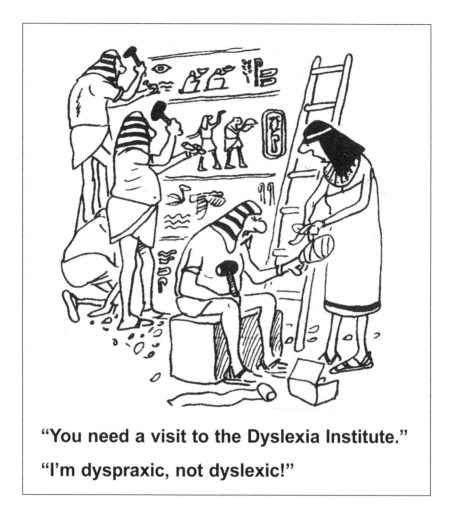

"You need a visit to the Dyslexia Institute."

"I'm dyspraxic, not dyslexic!"

everyone gets as a matter of course. Having to justify why you want something. Having to be seen to be better than your colleagues, even though people tell you that you've no need to. Having to be a 'shining example' all the time, as someone who's achieved something from way down the bowels of the earth. (Laughter)."

In the 1970s Black students were disproportionately placed in educationally subnormal (ESN) schools. Now, according to the DfES (Department for Education and Skills), Black Caribbean pupils are on average three times more likely to be permanently excluded from school than white pupils. At the peak of exclusions in the1990s the figures were much higher, varying from 4 to 15 times more likely to be excluded.

In her book 'Why Pick On Me? School Exclusion and Black Youth', published in 2001, Maud Blair refers to a CRE (Commission for Racial Equality) report: "At the time of writing this book, Black students in certain local education authorities were **nineteen** times more likely to be excluded than their white counterparts."

Research has shown that only about 15% of permanently excluded young people are taken back into mainstream schools. There is little alternative educational provision after exclusion and this leads to some getting involved in criminal activities.

This then needs to be seen alongside the very large number of Black people in prison (proportionately eight times higher than white people in 2003), where up to 40% of the inmates are dyslexic. It is hard not to see a connection between racism, education and dyslexia.

In the past dyslexia was seen as a white middle-class condition, partly because psychologists felt more confident that they could exclude other obvious causes of reading failure. Nearly all the books on dyslexia are written by white middle-class authors who are non-dyslexic. The vast majority are academic, in small print and with no pictures! In other words they are not written for dyslexics to read.

Dyslexia is a critical issue worldwide. There is widespread ignorance about it and the consequences can be devastating. There is an urgent need for more accessible information.

A CULTURAL PERSPECTIVE

"The question of how ethnicity and social or cultural factors affect those with dyslexia has not been explored in the literature."

Ellen Morgan & Cynthia Klein 'The Dyslexic Adult in a Non-Dyslexic World' 2000

■ ■ ■

"Every dyslexic is different. So too is every country, culture and educational context."

Ian Smythe, John Everatt & Robin Salter 'International Book of Dyslexia' 2004

■ ■ ■

"Discrimination suffered by dyslexic employees can be even worse if they are from an ethnic minority. Union representatives will need to be particularly careful to identify and challenge racial stereotyping."

Brian Hagan 'Dyslexia in the Workplace: A Guide for Unions' 2004

Culture is important because, although dyslexia has a neurological basis in the brain, it is through culture that dyslexia is experienced. Before reading and writing became so crucial, dyslexics were probably at an advantage. They are often strong visual thinkers, so they may have been better at hunting and constructing shelters. They could have been the experts in picture writing and cave paintings. Their skill at seeing patterns could well have made them into seers and prophets, as well as helping them to navigate by the stars.

On the other hand, with the invention of alphabetic writing and the growth in literacy, dyslexia became more of a disadvantage. The Protestant Reformation in Europe encouraged everyone to learn to read the bible. At the end of the seventeenth century, Sweden, for example, already had a high literacy rate and an illiterate person was not allowed to marry or to be a witness in court.

But another important aspect of a cultural perspective on dyslexia is the significance of dyslexics knowing about themselves. It is a

---

Why did cavemen draw pictures of hippopotamuses and rhinoceroses on walls?

Because they couldn't spell their names.

---

political issue. The Disability Movement has taught us about self-advocacy, independent living, taking control, and the fact that knowledge is power. We don't want the experts telling us who we are. We want to tell them!

This is not to say that research is not needed, but why can't it be done **by** dyslexics or **with** dyslexics, not just **on** dyslexics? There are advanced courses on dyslexia being taught solely by non-dyslexics, with all the students being non-dyslexic. Some universities have even prevented dyslexic students from joining their teacher training courses.

We don't know exactly how dyslexia is viewed in the Black communities. But there is a clear need to raise awareness of the issues involved, just as there is in the rest of society and around the world. Hopefully this book will make a start by profiling the experience of a number of Black figures and by trying to explain the complex and intriguing nature of dyslexia.

WHO IS DYSLEXIC?

10% of people are dyslexic (1 in 10)

■ ■ ■

"Cultural influences can be seen in the strikingly different behavioural manifestations of dyslexia in different countries."

Uta Frith 'Brain, Mind and Behaviour in Dyslexia' 1997

■ ■ ■

"Family members of individuals with dyslexia have roughly a 50% chance of being dyslexic. Girls are just as likely to be dyslexic as boys."

Joanna Kellogg Uhry & Diana Brewster Clark 'Dyslexia: Theory and Practice of Instruction' 2005

■ ■ ■

Statistics vary, but the generally accepted view is that 10% of people in the UK are dyslexic, with 4% being severely dyslexic. This amounts to 6 million dyslexic individuals, with about 3 in every school class. It illustrates the fact that dyslexia is experienced on a spectrum, from severe to moderate to mild. In the European Union over 46 million people are affected by dyslexia. In Nigeria 14 million. In the world 650 million.

It is also the case that dyslexia is often measured in different ways. A wider definition in the USA, where they tend to use the term 'learning disabilities', puts the figure of dyslexics at between 10% and 20%.

In some countries the estimated figures are lower, but this may well be because their languages are more dyslexia friendly and so dyslexics are not so readily diagnosed. Italian, for instance, is more regular than English. Most of the letters have a one-to-one correspondence with sounds and can be taught separately, so Italian children tend to learn to read and spell very quickly.

Spanish, Greek, Welsh and most of the South African languages are also more regular and so present fewer problems than, for example, French or Polish. In English the main obstacle for

---

Mother: "Our new house is flawless!"

Daughter: "What will we walk on?"

---

dyslexics in processing language is the relationship between sound and symbol, between the spoken word and the written word - what is called phonological awareness.

In Chinese and Japanese, with their logographic scripts, the problems are more in the visual area and related to meaning, for instance writing 'shoe' when asked to spell 'boot'. But even in Chinese, their visual symbols or characters contain a phonetic element that aids pronunciation. Recent research in mainland China has found 4% - 8% of Mandarin-speaking school children to be dyslexic. When reading English, Chinese people tend to adopt a visual, whole-word strategy, so their dyslexia may only be discovered when they are asked to read unfamiliar words.

This all shows the importance of culture and language in how dyslexia is experienced. In the first months of life we learn the basic sounds of our mother tongue and screen out others. This is why it is harder to learn a foreign language later in life. It is why English people have difficulty pronouncing the Scottish **ch** as in loch, or the Welsh **ll** in Llannelli.

It also illustrates how complex dyslexia is, and that there is no single way of assessing it. It is more difficult, for example, to assess bilingual pupils.

DYSLEXICS IN PRISON

40% of prisoners are dyslexic (2 out of 5)
40% of the unemployed are dyslexic (2 out of 5)

■ ■ ■

"When I left Stowe in 1967, aged almost 17, my headmaster's parting words were: 'Congratulations, Branson. I predict you will go to prison or become a millionaire.'"

Richard Branson 'My Story' 1998

■ ■ ■

"The incidence of dyslexia in the prison population is between three to four times that found in the general population."

John Rack 'The Incidence of Hidden Disabilities in the Prison Population' 2005

■ ■ ■

Research on prisoners who are dyslexic has thrown up a variety of results, some claiming 50% or over. This has been due to different research methods and different definitions of dyslexia.

The British Dyslexia Association has carried out two recent studies of dyslexia in juvenile offenders. The first (2004), using a small sample, was carried out in collaboration with the Bradford Youth Offending Team and found 52% dyslexics. The second (2005) involved a larger group of 200, aged 15-17, at Wetherby Young Offender Institution, using computer based tests. The results indicated that about 31% of young offenders have dyslexia.

Cartoon by dyslexic artist Mike Juggins

The largest recent research was carried out in Yorkshire and Humberside, headed by John Rack of the Dyslexia Institute, and published in 2005. They interviewed 357 prisoners across 8 different categories of prison. The assessment procedures which they used were to find out those who were severely dyslexic, producing results ranging from 14% to 21%. This would imply that up to 40% could be dyslexic to some degree.

John Rack explains the hypothesis behind these figures and the importance of early diagnosis of dyslexia: "If proper support is not provided at school for someone who is dyslexic, then there is a greater risk of failure and perhaps antisocial behaviour arising out of frustration. This, in turn, could lead to social exclusion and an increased risk of offending." The Dyspel programme in London found that fewer than 5% of prisoners had their dyslexia identified at school.

What did the beaver say to the tree?

Nice gnawing you.

ECONOMIC COST

"Dyslexia is often described as the 'hidden disability' but it affects up to 2.9 million workers in the UK today."

Brian Hagan 'Dyslexia in the Workplace: A Guide for Unions' 2004

■ ■ ■

"In contrast to the high public awareness of dyslexia in German children, the existence of dyslexia in adults has been ignored."

'International Book of Dyslexia' 2004

■ ■ ■

- **50% of permanent school exclusions are dyslexic (1 in 2)**
- **2% of university students are dyslexic (1 in 50)**
- **25% of students at the Royal College of Art are dyslexic (1 in 4)**

More is now being done to assess school pupils for dyslexia, but it is still the case than up to 40% are still not diagnosed till after they leave school. Figures from the DfES in June 2005 show that 64% of children permanently excluded from school have special needs and at least 80% of those – that is, about 5,000 children – have dyslexia. The National Foundation for Education Research has calculated that it costs almost £50 million each year to support these children outside the school system.

The economic costs of not recognising and dealing with dyslexia are enormous. The Government states that poor literacy, language and numeracy skills have been estimated to cost this country "in excess of £10 billion a year". The Dyslexia Institute estimates that undiagnosed dyslexia costs the economy around £1 billion each year. According to the DfES publication 'A

'Little leaks sink £he ship'

by Mike Juggins

**You shouldn't
send a knight
out on a dog
like this!**

Framework for Understanding Dyslexia' (2004):
"Adults with poor literacy and numeracy skills
could earn up to £50,000 less over a lifetime and
are more likely to have health problems, live in a
disadvantaged area or be unemployed."

Yet the Government does not prioritise or
fund specialist teacher training. The British
Dyslexia Association has accredited courses for
professionals working in the field of dyslexia

and other specific learning difficulties. However, 65% of teachers attending these courses have to fund themselves.

The Dyslexia Institute estimates that with an investment of £27 million in training and teaching for primary schools, no child would be left behind and many problems would be avoided.

As Baroness Walmsley said in the House of Lords Dyslexia Debate on 7 December, 2005: "When you consider the £50 million savings on children who are excluded and the Dyslexia Institute's estimate that undiagnosed dyslexia costs the economy £1 billion every year, let alone the costs that could be avoided in the prison system, it seems amazing that the Government are not jumping at the chance of spending a tiny proportion of that - £27 million - as a good investment."

FAMOUS CONTEMPORARY DYSLEXICS

"It has become increasingly clear in recent years that dyslexics themselves are frequently endowed with high talent in many areas. Many dyslexics have superior talents in certain areas of non-verbal skill, such as art, architecture, engineering and athletics."

Norman Geschwind 'Address to the Orton Dyslexia Society' 1982

"Being dyslexic, I don't like to read. As a child I read train timetables instead of the classics, and delighted in making imaginary perfect connections from one obscure town in Europe to another. This fascination gave me an excellent grasp of European geography."

Nicholas Negroponte (Director of the MIT Media Lab) 'Being Digital' 1995

■ ■ ■

Muhammad Ali

Up until recently, no one knew any famous dyslexics. Now, however, there is a veritable dyslexic hall of fame!

Famous people with dyslexia are not so reticent about 'coming out'. Many want to try and destroy the stigma attached to it and do something to help those who have not been so successful.

They come mainly from the fields of art and sport: actresses like Whoopi Goldberg and Susan Hampshire; actors such as Danny Glover and Tom Cruise; Muhammad Ali and the basketball star Magic Johnson; the champion racing driver Jackie Stewart and Olympic swimmer Duncan Goodhew, who was called 'Duncan the Dunce' at school. Similarly Richard Rogers, the architect, was told at the age of 16: "The most you can expect is to be a policeman in South Africa." A very high proportion of architects are dyslexic.

Danny Glover was doubly mocked, because of his race and dyslexia: "Kids made fun of me because I was dark-skinned, had a wide nose and was dyslexic. Even as an actor, it took me a long time to realize why words and letters got jumbled in my mind and came out differently."

Who designed Noah's ark?

An ark-itect.

WHOOPI GOLDBERG

Whoopi Goldberg was born on 13 November 1955 in Manhattan, New York. Her original name was Caryn Elaine Johnson. She grew up speaking a "smattering of Greek, Italian, Spanish, Indian, Chinese, Yiddish".

She started acting at the age of eight in a children's theatre. But at school she was regarded as retarded and she dropped out of high school after only two weeks.

She only realised she was dyslexic when she was a grown woman: "When I was a kid they didn't call it dyslexia. They called it… you know, you were slow, or you were retarded, or whatever."

The consequences, however, were long-lasting: "What you can never change is the effect that the words **dumb** and **stupid** have on young people. So we must always be vigilant when those two words get stuck in our throat. 'Hey, dummy! God, you're stupid.' You know. Just remember that what those leave you with are forever."

She overcame this labelling with the help of her mother and other people's positive encouragement: "I knew I wasn't stupid, and I knew I wasn't dumb. My mother told me that. Everybody told me I wasn't stupid or dumb. If you

Whoopi Goldberg as Celie in the 1985 film, 'The Color Purple'

read to me, I could tell you everything that you read. They didn't know what it was. They knew I wasn't lazy, but what was it?"

In 1985 Whoopi Goldberg became world famous playing the part of Celie in Spielberg's film version of Alice Walker's 'The Color Purple'. She has since appeared in many films and shows, won an Oscar and hosted the Academy Awards several times. She is also a political activist, campaigning on issues such as gay rights, the homeless, children, human rights, drugs and the battle against AIDS. She has won the Hans Christian Andersen Award for Outstanding Achievement by a Dyslexic.

In 1997 she published her autobiography called 'Book'. She refers to the difficulties in writing it, as she usually works out all her material in her head: "Most people put pen to paper, but I've never been that kind of writer. I have to work my shit out on my feet, and then, after I've done it, I can finally set it down. But that's not how you write a book. I tried. I know."

She tried doing it orally, talking about herself, and produced "two wonderful transcripts". But as she recalls: "The transcripts didn't at all represent what I wanted this book to be. Finally it was suggested I find someone to help me organize all this material."

Initially she thought she didn't want anybody's help, but eventually she came round to the idea: "Suddenly the idea of having someone come and help me organize what was in my head and in these transcripts seemed not such a bad idea after all."

Her ghost writer, Dan Paisner, told her that she had to have some sort of structure and she took his advice: "So not only was I receiving some help in structuring the material, but I was revisiting it, and enlarging it, and creating new material.

Why are vampires thin?

They eat necks to nothing.

Mostly, though, what I was doing was learning, and there's nothing wrong with learning."

Finally she realised that the dyslexia which produces the weak structuring may also be what produces the comic genius of Whoopi Goldberg. Perhaps it wouldn't be such a good idea to become a conventional writer: "In about twenty-five years – maybe I will have learned how to write by then, like a formal essayist, but I don't know if that will be a good thing. I might really prefer to have someone take the craziness out of my head and organize it in a way that people can follow, because I really do believe I'm some sort of alien."

Little wonder that when she wrote a children's book called 'Alice', the two main characters show signs of dyslexia. The story is about Alice and her friends Robin and an invisible rabbit from Italy, named Salvador De Rabbit. They are travelling round New York and look for a map, but then they realise that it's not such a good idea: "Now Alice assumed that Robin could read a map, and Robin assumed that Alice could read a map. Truth was, neither Robin nor Alice could, so when they actually found one, they were pretty stumped." Finally the rabbit solves the problem by suggesting they go on the subway!

HARRY BELAFONTE

Harry Belafonte was born on 1 March, 1927 in New York. His mother was a mixed-race Jamaican and his father was also mixed-race, from Martinique. At the age of 8 he moved to Jamaica and then in 1940 returned to New York. His schooling was very disrupted, split between Kingston and Harlem. He finally dropped out after the ninth grade.

Harry Belafonte with his daughter Adrienne

Before becoming a singer and actor, he joined the Navy, where one day he was handed a copy of 'Color and Democracy' by W.E.B. Du Bois. He struggled with the words, spending hours poring over a single paragraph.

He recalls also how he did not understand the convention of footnotes and the fact that **ibid** (short for **ibidem**) means the same book as the one mentioned before: "I discovered that at the end of some sentences there was a number, and if you looked at the foot of the page the reference was to what it was all about – what source Du Bois gleaned this information from. So when I was on leave, going into Chicago, I went to a library with a long list of books.

"The librarian said, 'That's too many, young man. You're going to have to cut it down.'

"I said, 'I can make it very easy. Just give me everything you got by Ibid.'

"She said, 'There's no such writer.'

"I called her a racist. I said, 'Are you trying to keep me in darkness?' And I walked out of there angry."

The bridge player said: "Four spades: that's how ibidem."

Harry Belafonte eventually went to study at Piscator's New York Drama Workshop. Another student there at the time was fellow dyslexic Marlon Brando.

His future wife was studying for a PhD in child psychology. Harry recalls: "I kept telling her I was a real good subject for her because I was a retarded child with lots of problems."

On 15 February 2003, 12 million people worldwide demonstrated against the Iraq War, which according to the Guinness Book of Records was "the largest mass protest in history". Half a million protested in New York and on the podium was Harry Belafonte wearing a blue button on his overcoat saying 'The World Says No to War'. He said, "America is a vast and diverse country and we are part of the greater truth that makes our nation. We stand for peace, for the truth of what is at the heart of the American people."

Next to him was fellow dyslexic Danny Glover who also addressed the crowd. He spoke of earlier heroes such as Sojourner Truth, Harriet Tubman and Paul Robeson, and then proclaimed, "We stand here today because our right to dissent and our right to participate in a real democracy has been hijacked by those who call for war. We stand at this threshold of history and we say 'Not In Our Name'!"

GARTH VAZ

Garth Vaz was born on 5 October 1947 in the village of Bluefields, in the parish of Westmoreland, in Jamaica. His remarkable story is told by his brother A. McDonald Vaz in his book 'The Doctor He Begged to Be', published in 1996, which begins, "This book is written about a dyslexic, by a dyslexic, for the dyslexic and others who have learning problems with the conventional approach." It took him five years to write it.

At the age of four Garth said, "I am going to be a doctor someday." But it was to take enormous courage and persistence to achieve his aim. At the age of seven, according to his brother, "His ABC consisted of just three letters. He counted from one to forty but left out thirty-eight numbers along the way." On his first day at school "he spent most of his time daydreaming and staring into space".

At the age of eleven his parents split up and he went with his mother, brother and two sisters to live in the village of Darliston, near Savanna-la-Mar. The house had no electricity or running water and it was Garth's job to fetch water and firewood, and to clear the land to plant yam, cassava and corn. At the age of fourteen he was travelling round the country selling religious and medical books to raise money for the family.

Garth Vaz

In those days you had to pay to go to high school, so Garth spent two years earning money as a car mechanic to pay the fees. When he finally got to the school in Mandeville, he dropped out after nine weeks.

In 1967 he left for the USA and eventually graduated from Ocala Junior College. He started classes at the University of Florida, but again after nine weeks dropped out. By that time he was married and was told by his wife that he didn't "have enough brains to make it in a university setting". Similarly his father-in-law said, "Man you will never make it."

His brother describes the difficulties Garth was having taking exams: "He would read the question from the test paper incorrectly. As a result, he would write down the wrong answer. His second dilemma was that sometimes he would read the question correctly, but by the time it was processed in his head and got to the paper, the

A. McDonald Vaz

answer would be incorrect. His next problem was the time element. He never could finish on time, and that brought other complications. The knowledge that fellow students were finishing when he was nowhere close to completing added further frustrations and distractions."

He got accepted again in the University of Florida College of Medicine, but was held back for two years and kicked out three times, before finally graduating in 1989. He suffered racism and prejudice because of his dyslexia, which was only diagnosed two years before he graduated. He then got a job in the University Hospital in Jacksonville and finally became a doctor in Gonzales, Texas.

His brother explains the importance of those early days as a car mechanic, "Auto mechanics definitely prepared Garth for a greater sophistication – the human body. He developed the skill to diagnose and troubleshoot gas, diesel and electric motors. As a dyslexic it was not imperative, but it was very important for him to have matured in the auto mechanic field before approaching the human body."

He adds, "Unscrewing a simple nut can be mind boggling to the dyslexic when he is first introduced to auto mechanics. But that same dyslexic, if given the right intellectual exposure, could go on to develop the greatest scientific invention."

The book which tells Garth's story begins and ends with the day he graduated and phoned his brother:

"In reaching for the phone I said, 'Wa hapin sah?'

He responded, 'Bouy dem decide fi let me out a here.'

My response was, 'OK, Dr Vaz.' I guess that was another way of saying congratulations."

FAMOUS DYSLEXICS FROM THE PAST

"Imagination is more important than knowledge. Knowledge is limited. Imagination encircles the world."

Albert Einstein, 1929

■ ■ ■

Once famous contemporary dyslexics had been identified, it was a small step to suggest famous figures from the past who could have been dyslexic. It is of course impossible to prove, but there are many signs which indicate dyslexia in some very celebrated people.

It has been suggested, for example, that the famous French novelist, Gustave Flaubert (1821-1880), who wrote 'Madame Bovary', was dyslexic. His niece Caroline commented on his language processing difficulties: "Having made a strenuous effort to understand the symbols he could make nothing of, he wept giant tears. For a long time he could not understand the elementary connection that made of two letters one syllable, of several syllables a word."

Significantly, when he was fifteen, Flaubert wrote a novel about a character, half-man and half-monkey, who attracts the attention of scientists because he cannot learn to read. He cannot comprehend that the signs on the page stand for words. When examined by the scientists, he does not respond because, although he can talk, he is too frightened he will make a mistake.

In a letter to George Sand in 1866, Flaubert wrote: "**You** don't know what it is, to spend an entire day with your head in your hands, taxing your poor brain in search of a word. With you, the flow of ideas is broad, continuous, like a river. With me it's a tiny trickle. I can achieve a cascade only by the most arduous effort."

Similarly the Irish poet W. B. Yeats (1865-1939) had great difficulties with spelling, punctuation and reading: "Several of my uncles and aunts had tried to teach me to read, and because they could not, and because I was much older than children who read easily, had come to think that I had not all my faculties." His father reacted even more violently: "My father was an angry and impatient teacher and flung the reading book at my head."

Yeats found it hard to organise his ideas and put them down on paper: "My thoughts were a great excitement, but when I tried to do anything with them, it was like trying to park a balloon in a

Galileo went up the Leaning Tower of Pisa and dropped things down. This is how we discovered what is now called gravy.

shed in a high wind." He eventually won the Nobel Prize for Literature in 1923, but never learned to spell!

Auguste Rodin (1840-1917), the French sculptor who created 'The Thinker' and 'The Kiss', was the worst pupil in his Jesuit primary school. He was bullied and called stupid because of his slow reactions. He showed no interest in reading or writing: "I learned practically nothing. With me everything was observed empirically, was lived; everything sprang from my love of nature and of

Rodin, self-portrait in charcoal (left) and Rodin's 'The Thinker'

the life around me. I had to work with the patience of a worm, moving gradually from place to place in complete darkness; for I knew nothing."

He then went to a private school in Beauvais, but left at 13, still virtually illiterate. He echoes many dyslexics' view of school: "I always felt that I was being held in prison." He was capable of intense application and long, hard work, but spelling remained a mystery to him throughout his life. He dictated all his letters to secretaries. As Rodin wisely concluded: "Faults in spelling matter less than faults in drawing."

LEONARDO DA VINCI (1452-1519)

Perhaps the most famous of all is Leonardo da Vinci, artist, designer, inventor and scientist. He was born on 15 April 1452 in Vinci, near Florence. Leonardo was illegitimate. His mother was a peasant maid, but he was brought up by his father, who was a notary, and his stepmother.

Leonardo Da Vinci, self-portrait

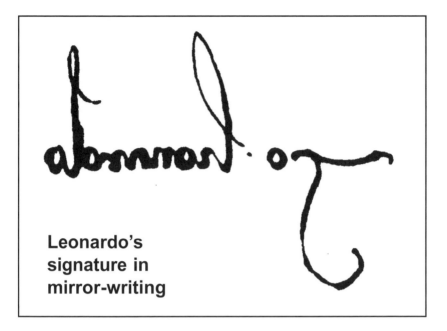

Leonardo's signature in mirror-writing

He was left-handed, which would normally have been 'corrected' at the time, if he had gone to school – but there is no evidence that he went to school. He thought in pictures first and then had to deconstruct the image into writing. Most of the time he wrote his notes and journals backwards, from right to left, in mirror image. This is a trait shared by some left-handed dyslexic people and often they are not even conscious that they are writing in this way.

Over 7,000 pages of his notebooks have survived, filled with drawings and ideas, but he could never put them in order, and connected ideas would crop up on several different pages. This difficulty with structuring and ordering material is another characteristic of dyslexia.

Leonardo called himself a "man without letters", without an adequate knowledge of Greek and Latin. His spelling was bizarre, despite Italian being phonetically regular, and even when he was copying from other texts. But as he said: "You should prefer a good scientist without literary abilities to a literate one without scientific skills."

He began many things without finishing them and was notoriously slow, taking three years (1495-8), for example, to paint the 'Last Supper' in Milan. At times he would remain in the room for three or four days without touching the picture, only coming for a few hours to remain before it, with folded arms, gazing at the figures as if to criticise himself.

He took four years (1503-7) over the 'Mona Lisa'. While he was drawing her portrait he engaged people to play and sing, and jesters to keep her merry. As Leonardo said: "Men of genius really are doing most when they work least, or they are thinking out ideas and perfecting the conception, which they subsequently carry out with their hands." He often gave up painting to concentrate on mathematical experiments.

Leonardo certainly had an innovative mind, being able to make connections between many different fields of knowledge. He was a lateral

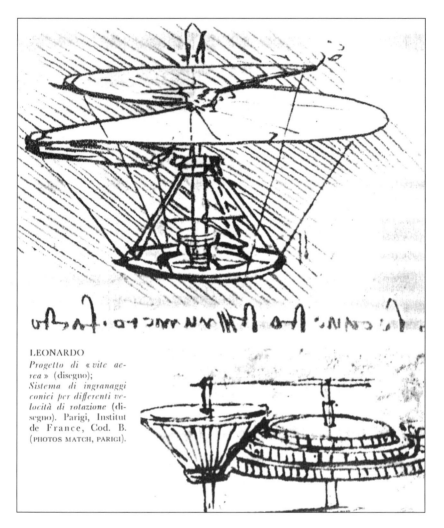

LEONARDO
Progetto di « vite ae-
rea » (disegno);
Sistema di ingranaggi
conici per differenti ve-
locità di rotazione (disegno). Parigi, Institut
de France, Cod. B.
(PHOTOS MATCH, PARIGI).

Leonardo's helicopter design

thinker, enabling him to invent the self-sealing gate for a canal lock, for example, which is still in use today, simply by rotating the triangular arch from the architecture of buildings.

He was intrigued by the idea of human flight and made numerous sketches of flying machines.

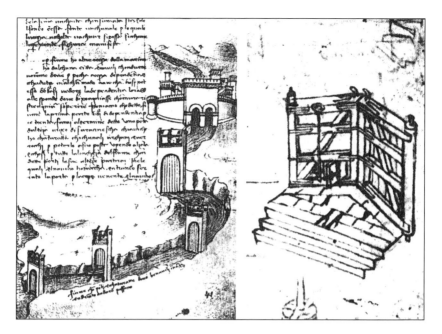

Leonardo's design for a canal lock

He describes one sketch, which looks like a helicopter: "A small model can be made of paper with a spring like metal shaft that after having been released, after having been twisted, causes the screw to spin up into the air."

HANS CHRISTIAN ANDERSEN (1805-1875)

One of the most famous inventors of fairy tales in the world is Hans Christian Andersen. He wrote 'The Princess and the Pea', 'The Little Mermaid', 'The Snow Queen' and 'The Emperor's New Suit', among scores of others. During his lifetime he was celebrated throughout Europe, but his early life was a real struggle.

Hans Christian Andersen

He was born on 2 April 1805 in Odense, Denmark, where he first went to school: "I went to the Poor School where all I learned was religion, writing and arithmetic and not much of the latter. I was scarcely able to spell one word correctly."

Later he spent nearly four years at Slagelse Grammar School and describes the experience in his autobiography: "I wanted to learn, but I was just groping. I behaved like a person who cannot swim and has been thrown into the sea; it was a question of life and death for me to keep up, but the waves poured over me: one was called mathematics, another grammar, another geography, etc. – I felt overwhelmed and afraid that I would never get through them."

The headmaster told him he was "stupid" and he lost more and more of his self-confidence: "For me, to be made ridiculous was the most dreadful thing, and thus at the start of every lesson, when the headmaster came in, I was all but paralysed with terror and that made my answers the opposite of what they should have been."

Hans Christian Andersen was bullied and made fun of by fellow-pupils, as well as by

Which cheese is made backwards?

Edam.

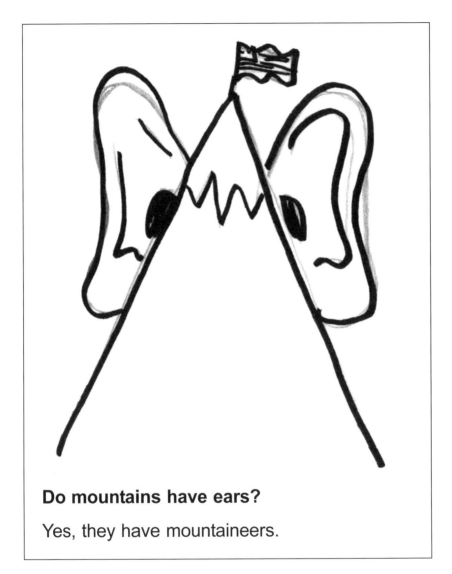

Do mountains have ears?

Yes, they have mountaineers.

teachers, a parallel with his story 'The Ugly Duckling'. When he finally went to say goodbye to the headmaster and thank him, "his parting words were that I would never get to the university, that the verses I wrote, if they ever got printed, would lie and rot as waste paper in the bookseller's loft, while I would end in the madhouse."

He found grammar and spelling very difficult: "All grammar is hard to me and when I get anxious about it, the blood flies to my head at once and I give stupid answers."

Another indication of dyslexia is his literal thinking and lack of understanding of certain conventions. On his first visit to Copenhagen, at the age of 14, he was walking by the theatre when a tout stopped him and asked him if he wanted a ticket. He describes his response: "I was so ignorant of the world and of the ways of the city that I thought he wanted to make me a present of a ticket, and I thanked him so cordially that he thought I was making a fool of him and became angry, with the result that I ran in terror from the place."

In 1857 he visited England and stayed for a while with Charles Dickens. Andersen records in his diary that he had "brackfest" with Dickens and his wife. Dickens thought Andersen could not even speak his own language properly and made it clear to various people that he considered him rather stupid.

ALBERT EINSTEIN (1879-1955)

Einstein is probably the one scientist everyone has heard of. His name is synonymous with brains and intelligence. He invented the theory of relativity, which he visualised before writing it down. Yet his start in life was not so promising.

Albert Einstein

He was born on 14 March 1879 in Ulm, in southern Germany, of middle-class Jewish parents, though after his first year they moved to Munich.

Einstein was slow in learning to talk: "It is true that my parents were worried because I began to speak relatively late, so much so that they consulted a doctor. I can't say how old I was then, certainly not less than three."

As a child he had difficulty processing language, which is a key element of dyslexia. His acquisition of language seemed laborious and self-conscious, compared to the natural way in which most children learn language. If someone asked him a question, he would first form the answer in his head, try it out in an undertone – deliberately, with obvious lip movements – and only after assuring himself that his formulation was correct would he repeat the sentence aloud. This often gave the impression that he was saying everything twice, and the maidservant therefore called him "stupid". He only gave up this habit when he was about eight years old.

He heard words before he wrote them, and only when they sounded right did he put them down on paper. He commented to an interviewer: "I am the acoustic type. I learn by ear and give by word. Writing is difficult."

As a young boy, Einstein was prone to violent tantrums and he also objected to the strict discipline of school: "The teachers at the elementary school seemed to me like drill sergeants, and the teachers at the high school like lieutenants."

Although he was generally an able student at high school, Einstein had specific difficulties with memory and words: "My principal weakness was a bad memory, especially a bad memory for words and texts."

At the age of 60, he recollected how much he detested the "mindless and mechanical method of teaching, which, because of my poor memory for words, caused me great difficulties, which it seemed to me pointless to overcome. I would rather let all kinds of punishment descend on me than learn to rattle something off by heart." One of his teachers told him: "You will never amount to anything, Einstein."

He finally left school at 15 on his own initiative, without taking the final exam, and joined his parents in Milan. He summed up his view of

---

Why is it dangerous to do maths in the jungle?

Because if you add 4 and 4, you get ate.

school, stressing the way in which it can undermine a pupil's self-confidence: "The worst of all, in my view, is when a school is mainly run by fear, power and artificial authority. Such treatment destroys the healthy feelings, the integrity and self-confidence of the pupils."

Einstein eventually went to study at Zurich Polytechnic. But even there, where his brilliance at science and mathematics was becoming clear, one professor described him as a "lazy dog" who "never bothered about mathematics at all". His physics teacher, while admitting Einstein's intelligence, remarked: "But you have one fault: no one can tell you anything."

A characteristic of dyslexia is the need to work ten times harder at a task to succeed, which contrast vividly with the stereotype of laziness. Einstein points this out when referring to his success: "I know perfectly well that I myself have no special talents. It was curiosity, obsession, and sheer perseverance that brought me to my ideas."

He also explains his method of thinking – without words: "The words or the language, as they are written or spoken, do not seem to play any role in my mechanism of thought. The psychical entities which seem to serve as elements in thought are certain signs and more or less clear images which can be 'voluntarily' reproduced and combined."

It is like a visual game: "This combinatory play seems to be the essential feature in productive thought – before there is any connection with logical construction in words or other kinds of signs which can be communicated to others." He would only use words after this "associative play is sufficiently established".

Like Leonardo da Vinci, Einstein saw the importance of wondering and slowness, in a world that seems always to value certainty and speed. Near the end of his life he explained why he discovered the theory of relativity rather than anyone else: "An adult does not reflect on space-time problems. Anything that needs reflection on this matter he believes he did in his early childhood. I, on the other hand, developed so slowly that I only began to reflect about space and time when I was grown up. Naturally I then penetrated more deeply into these problems than an ordinary child would."

PABLO PICASSO (1881-1973)

Born in Malaga, southern Spain, on 25 October 1881, Picasso was one of the greatest artists of the twentieth century. He recalled that he could draw long before he could talk.

Pablo Picasso

He also had school phobia. The family maid had to drag him through the streets to school by brute force amid noisy, terrible scenes. He was then sent to a private school where his spelling was very idiosyncratic and he was slow at both reading and mathematics.

Picasso had trouble staying in his seat and would often leave the classroom and wander out to the kitchen where he followed the headmaster's wife about. When he did stay in class, he was usually totally paralysed. He heard nothing and learnt nothing.

He would watch the clock and repeat, "At one o'clock, at one o'clock." Sometimes he discovered that he had been chanting these words aloud in a sing-song voice, to the other pupils' amusement. He later recalled, "I stared at the clock like an idiot, eyes raised, head sideways."

His difficulty in paying attention was partly related to language processing, as he was concentrating on the **process** of paying attention, rather than the **purpose** of paying attention: "You can't imagine what I suffered trying to pay

---

Why were the early days of history called the dark ages?

Because there were so many knights.

---

attention. As soon as I began thinking that I had to pay attention, I'd be distracted by the thought that it was necessary to pay attention, and this would confuse me."

Sometimes, like many dyslexics before and since, Picasso would just stare out of the schoolroom window. He would then try and copy everything he saw, in crayon, all over his textbooks.

He describes how he tried to learn arithmetic: "One and one, two... Two and one... etc. It never sank in. Don't think I didn't try. I tried hard to concentrate. I used to say to myself, now I'm going to pay attention. Let's see. Two and one. One o'clock... Ah! That's not it. And I would start all over again from the beginning, but immediately I'd be lost, absorbed in the thought of the hour for going home, of whether they would or would not come to get me. Then I would get up and go to the toilet or some other place, without bothering to ask permission."

His weakness in maths was because he saw numbers as shapes, representing objects, rather than as abstract symbols. On the way home from a maths exam which he couldn't do, he imagined the pigeon he would paint when he got home: "The little eye of the pigeon is round like a 0. Under the 0 a 6, and under that a 3. The eyes are like 2's, and so are the wings. The little feet rest on the table, as if on a horizontal line… underneath it all the total." In the same way he saw the hidden potential in junk items, which he cleverly turned into sculptures.

At the age of 10 Picasso was virtually unable to read or write, but there are other ways of recording your thoughts and feelings, as he later said, "Painting is just another way of keeping a diary." Even at the age of 17 he could barely read, but by that age he was well on the way to becoming the most innovative artist of the twentieth century.

AGATHA CHRISTIE (1890-1976)

Agatha Christie is the largest selling author in the world, with sales of well over 2 billion, translated into 104 languages. She wrote 78 crime novels and 150 short stories, and is also very well-known for television productions featuring her famous detectives, Hercule Poirot and Miss Marple.

Agatha Christie

She was born Agatha Miller on 15 September 1890 in Torquay, Devon. Her schooling was very patchy and her mother thought that "no child ought to be allowed to read until it was eight years old: better for the eyes and also for the brain". But Agatha taught herself to read before she was five, by using sight vocabulary, rather than phonics.

As she explains in her autobiography, she would produce "lines of shaky B's and R's, which I seem to have had great difficulty in distinguishing since I had learned to read by the look of **words** and not by their letters". She enjoyed herself "far more with figures than with the recalcitrant letters of the alphabet". In fact her main loves were mathematics and music.

At home Agatha was always seen as slow, though she realised later that the family standard of speed had been unusually high: "I myself was always recognised, though quite kindly, as 'the slow one' of the family. The reactions of my mother and my sister were unusually quick – I could never keep up. I was, too, very inarticulate. It was always difficult for me to assemble into words what I wanted to say. 'Agatha is always so terribly **slow**' was always the cry."

She constantly refers to her inability to spell: "Writing and spelling were always terribly difficult for me." Her first written story was "very short, since both writing and spelling were a pain to me".

Agatha Christie as a girl

The problem remained throughout her life: "I was still an extraordinary bad speller and have remained so until the present day."

Grammar she also found incomprehensible: "Grammar I could not understand in the least: I could not see **why** certain things were called prepositions or what verbs were supposed to **do**, and the whole thing was a foreign language to me." Similarly with French which she learnt by talking: "As regards French grammar and spelling I was practically in the bottom class."

Sometimes she would confuse words, such as compliment and complement, and she gives an amusing example of such a dyslexism when she was seven years old. She had grazed her arm and her mother told her not to cry, but to be brave like a soldier: "My answer was to bawl out: 'I don't want to be a brave soldier. I want to be a cowyard!'"

Agatha's mother eventually sent her to school, but she never stayed in one for longer than 18 months. She recollects how, in a girls' school in Torquay, even in a subject which she was good at, she could be reduced to confusion by the exam system: "I remember now that at an arithmetic exam at Miss Guyer's school I had come out bottom, though I had been top of the class all the week previously. Somehow, when I read the questions at the exam, my mind shut up and I was unable to think."

A similar feeling overcame her when she was writing her first detective story. She had settled the beginning and end, but it was still "all in a tangle". She became absent-minded and forgetful and got very tired and cross: "Writing has that effect, I find. Also, as I began to be enmeshed in the middle part of the book, the complications got the better of me instead of my being the master of them."

Lateral thinking or digression is often seen as a characteristic of dyslexia and at school Agatha was "severely criticised for not keeping to the subject". She gives the example of writing a story about autumn which somehow later turned into a story about a pig, without any obvious connection.

Agatha Christie wanted to write under the pseudonym of Martin West, because she thought people would be prejudiced against a woman writing detective stories. Her publisher persuaded her to keep her own name, which he thought was very distinctive. It is also interesting to note that she usually worked out all the plot details and clues in her head before putting pen to paper. This is the way many dyslexic writers work.

Fish monger's
FRESH FISH

Why are fishmongers so mean?

Because their job makes them sell-fish.

She confesses that she was "a terribly shy person" and says, "I knew that I was not very good at anything." She writes: "Inarticulate I shall always be. It is probably one of the causes that have made me a writer."

This lack of public confidence could be tackled through time, which dyslexics usually can't get enough of: "I must give myself time to look at a problem carefully before deciding how I would deal with it." This is why she valued the freedom of her childhood: "I began to appreciate time. There is nothing more wonderful to have in one's life, than time. I don't believe people get enough of it nowadays. I was excessively fortunate in my childhood and youth, just **because** I had so much time."

Like Leonardo with his painting, it was time that she valued so much as a writer: "The most blessed thing about being an author is that you do it in private and **in your own time**. It can worry you, bother you, give you a headache; you can go nearly mad trying to arrange your plot in the way it should go and you know it could go; **but** – you do not have to stand up and make a fool of yourself in public."

HISTORY AND THEORY

"History comes out of the struggles of real people, their families, their needs, their agonies, their hopes."

Danny Glover 2006

■ ■ ■

The word **dyslexia** comes from the Greek, meaning difficulty with words or language. It was first used in Germany in the 1880s by Professor Rudolf Berlin of Stuttgart, who described it as a peculiar form of word-blindness.

The same term, word-blindness, was used in Britain by Dr Pringle Morgan, a general medical practitioner working in Sussex, in his famous paper in the British Medical Journal in 1896. It was called 'A Case of Congenital Word Blindness'. The author describes a boy of 14, called Percy, who, although he had "been at school or under tutors since he was 7 years old", seemed unable to learn to read: "The schoolmaster who taught him for some years says that he would be the smartest lad

in the school if the instruction was entirely oral."
This discrepancy between obvious intelligence and
difficulty in reading was to remain one of the key
indicators of dyslexia.

Pringle Morgan writes: "In writing his name
he made a mistake, putting 'Precy' for 'Percy',
and he did not notice the mistake until his
attention was called to it more than once." He
then asked Percy to write a number of words,
which he wrote as follows:

song	**scone**
subject	**scojock**
without	**wichout**
English	**Englis**
shilling	**sening**
seashore	**seasow**

Pringle Morgan continues: "He was quite unable to
spell the name of his father's house, though he
must have seen it and spelt it scores of times. In
asking him to read the sentences he had just
written a short time previously he could not do so,
but made mistakes over every word except the
very simplest. Words such as 'and' and 'the' he
always recognises."

Percy was fond of arithmetic and found no
difficulty with it, but said that printed or written
words had no meaning to him: "He seems to have
no power of preserving and storing up the visual

Dr Pringle Morgan

impression produced by words – hence the words, though seen, have no significance for him. His visual memory for words is defective or absent; which is equivalent of saying that he is what Kussmaul has termed 'word blind'."

This case was particularly interesting to Pringle Morgan: "It is unique, so far as I know, in that it follows upon no injury or illness, but is evidently congenital." Nevertheless he recognised that some progress had been made through "laborious and persistent training". Percy, "by dint of constant application", had learnt his letters, and Pringle Morgan concludes by saying: "It will be interesting to see what effect further training will have on his condition."

JAMES HINSHELWOOD

James Hinshelwood, a Glasgow eye surgeon, was also studying the issue and influenced Dr Pringle Morgan, who wrote of Hinshelwood: "It was your paper – may I call it your classical paper? – on word-blindness and visual memory published in 'The Lancet' on December 21, 1895, which first drew my attention to this subject, and my reason

James Hinshelwood

for publishing this case was that there was no reference anywhere, so far as I knew, to the possibility of the condition being congenital."

In 'The Lancet' of 26 May 1900, Hinshelwood wrote again passionately on the subject, in a manner which is still relevant today: "I have little doubt that these cases of congenital word-blindness are by no means so rare as the absence of recorded cases would lead us to infer. Their rarity is, I think, accounted for by the fact that when they do occur, they are not recognised. It is a matter of the highest importance to recognise the cause and the true nature of this difficulty in learning to read which is experienced by these children, otherwise they may be harshly treated as imbeciles or incorrigibles, and either neglected or punished for a defect for which they are in no wise responsible. The recognition of the true character of the difficulty will lead the parents and teachers of these children to deal with them in the proper way, not by harsh and severe treatment, but by attempting to overcome the difficulty by patient and persistent training."

He refers to the fact that acquired word-blindness had been known about since the 1870s,

---

What letters are bad for your teeth?

D-K.

73

but that congenital word-blindness had a hereditary tendency. Also he points to its long history: "Cases of this defect have existed ever since men began to read by the aid of the twenty-two letters of the alphabet invented by the Phoenicians about 4,000 years ago."

In 1917 James Hinshelwood wrote up his ideas more fully in a book entitled 'Congenital Word-Blindness'. It confirms the prevalent view of the time that the difficulty was to do with visual processing. Again Hinshelwood expressed his opinion that patience and perseverance were needed to tackle the problem.

SAMUEL ORTON

Twenty years later Samuel Orton introduced the theory that it was language factors, rather than visual ones, which affected dyslexic children. In his book 'Reading, Writing and Speech Problems in Children', he called the condition strephosymbolia, which means a twisting of symbols . He realised that it was genetic, as it often ran in families, and also that it tended to be associated with other language problems.

Samuel Orton

Orton was a professor of neurology at Columbia University and carried out his research in the state of Iowa and in New York. When studying reading he found "a group of very considerable size in every school who suddenly meet a task which they cannot accomplish".

Not that they are unintelligent or lacking in creative ability: "Sometimes, indeed, a highly imaginative child will concoct a whole story bearing no relation to the words on the page before him beyond one or two initial or key words which he cleverly weaves into his own production." Nor that they are not interested in the contents of books: "Such children are usually avidly interested in stories, both those told to them and those read aloud."

He realised that, although they had difficulties with reading words, their "interpretation of pictorial and diagrammatic material is frequently very good". They also often had the skill of reading mirror writing. He describes one eleven-year-old girl who struggled with normal writing, but who could produce clear mirror writing.

In the children's spelling mistakes, Orton saw a pattern, particularly related to the "failure to repicture the exact order of the letters". Hence the common errors of putting 'saw' for 'was', 'form' for 'from', 'clam' for 'calm'. He also criticised the contemporary emphasis on the 'look and say'

What is a bear without an ear?

A 'b'.

method of teaching reading, giving examples of children reading 'laughter' as 'loiter', 'flock' as 'float', 'experiment' as 'experience'.

Orton stressed the devastating effect these difficulties had on children, especially if undiagnosed, and how they approach "every task with the expectation of failure". He writes of "a generalized feeling of depression" which develops, and "an attitude of extreme dejection".

This situation can be improved: "When an adequate program of retraining has been instituted and is proving to the child that he can make progress against his mysterious handicap, the inferiority feelings usually gradually evaporate." The teaching has to be tailor-made, as "each child presents an individual problem".

DENMARK

Also in the 1930s two divergent ways of looking at dyslexia developed in Denmark. On the one hand educational psychologists in the Board of Education in Copenhagen adopted a psychological approach. On the other hand Edith Norrie, who was dyslexic herself, used a more medical concept. In 1936 she opened a private institute at Hadersler which ran without any public support until 1948. She used the methods which had succeeded with her: teaching phonics, encouraging independent learning and the reading of books out of interest rather than duty.

Another Dane, the neurologist Knud Hermann, was also concerned about the effect the traditional educational system was having on dyslexic children. Hermann was chief physician at University Hospital in Copenhagen and, in his book 'Reading Disability', published in 1959, he writes that "word-blind persons are often unjustly treated, making them overtly nervous, discouraged and depressed". In their frustration they often turn to stealing, fighting and truancy: "Many word-blind sufferers in this state think of suicide, and suicidal attempts are not unknown."

Based on Swedish research, Hermann estimates 10% of the population to be dyslexic, but many remain undiagnosed: "There are still many who suffer as a result of their dyslexia, because the condition is discovered so late that it is difficult to give the individual effective help before he leaves school. It is unfortunately also true that there are teachers who either know nothing about word-blindness, or deny its very existence."

He realised the crucial importance of direction and sequence in a word and saw the connection between difficulties in spelling and directional uncertainty. Many dyslexics find it hard to tell left from right and have difficulty in orientation and map-reading.

The significance of phonics was stressed by Hermann. He points out that in English the letter 'a' can be used to depict 8 different sounds – any, glad, far, want, all, admit, came, village. This leads him to conclude: "It has often been said, and probably rightly, that the first fact of congenital word-blindness being first described in England was related to the non-phonetic constitution of written English."

He also points out that, although neurologists had been the first to diagnose dyslexia, a different approach was generally being taken by

---

Why did the pony cough?

He was a little hoarse.

---

psychologists: "In recent years, however, a high proportion of the studies of poor reading skills have been carried out, in this country at least, by educators and psychologists, and there has been a tendency to minimize brain physiology and to emphasize the environmental and emotional factors in learning."

Some psychiatrists had claimed that it was emotional disturbance which led to poor reading skills, whereas Hermann maintained that, in the case of word-blindness, it was the other way round – dyslexia was leading to emotional disturbance! He argued that if the psychological theory was right, then why did the problems always persist into adult life and were "never totally mastered". (In the same way, during this period, autism was thought to be caused by bad mothering and attempts were made to cure it by psychotherapy.)

Hermann makes a plea for interdisciplinary research: "It would seem desirable for investigators to cooperatively study poor reading and other language skills as functions of the brain – an organ which is the joint province of the anatomist, the neurologist, the psychologist, the psychiatrist, the geneticist, and the educator."

Have you ever seen a duchess?

Yes – it's exactly the same as an English 's'.

DYSLEXIA

The word dyslexia took a long time to be accepted, but in the 1960s it eventually took over from word-blindness. In 1966 the first local dyslexia association was set up in Bath and by 1970 there were eight of these associations in Britain. They then saw the need to establish a national association and consequently the British Dyslexia Association was formed in 1972.

The 1970s saw a heightened debate as to whether dyslexia really existed or not. The reluctance by many to acknowledge its biological root may have had something to do with the optimism of the 1960s and the industrial militancy

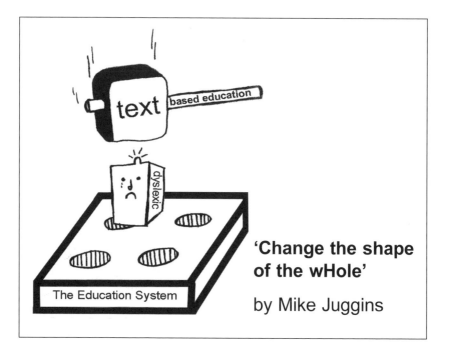

'Change the shape of the wHole'

by Mike Juggins

of the 1970s, with the Civil Rights movement and student revolt also playing a part. It was a time when social factors were seen as the determining force and it seemed possible to change the world. 'We shall overcome' was applied to dyslexia too!

As early as 1964, the neurologist Macdonald Critchley wrote: "What had hitherto been a medical province or responsibility now became invaded by sociologists and educational psychologists." He claims that neurologists have sometimes been at fault by allowing psychologists to assert that neurologists regard dyslexics as incurable. Critchley himself maintains that "the disability is one which is amenable to treatment provided this be carried out with sufficient intensity, patience, sympathy and understanding".

He anticipates decades of struggle to get dyslexia accepted: "Many educationalists appear sceptical as to whether developmental dyslexia occurs at all: some go further and proclaim outright that it is a myth." (As recently as September 2005, a Channel 4 'Dispatches' programme was broadcast, entitled 'The Dyslexia Myth') Critchley also states that "the blame has fallen on one scapegoat after another, the teacher, the parents, and the child".

Now that the scientific consensus supports the neurological basis of dyslexia, there is another debate to be had. Too often a medical model of

dyslexia implies that there is something wrong with the dyslexic that should be cured. An alternative model, which has been widely used in the Disability Movement, is that that it is society which makes disability a problem by not being inclusive and by not recognising how oppressive social norms can be.

Similarly there is a debate between theories of deficit and difference. Just as some theorists see working-class or Black language as deficient and inferior to standard English, so some people just see dyslexia as a deformed brain. As will have become clear from the examples in this book, it is our view that dyslexics have strengths as well as weaknesses and these strengths can contribute greatly to our culture and society.

WHAT IS DYSLEXIA?

"In the course of researching this book I have tried to find a single agreed definition of dyslexia. However, after discovering over 28 different ones and not even exhausting my search, I gave up."

Anita Keates 'Dyslexia and ICT' 2000

■ ■ ■

"Perhaps the most important gain that has already accrued from the uncontested demonstration that dyslexia has a strong genetic component is that this proves absolutely that dyslexia is a real neurological condition, and not a convenient word to be used by anxious mothers to hide their children's laziness or stupidity."

John Stein 'Dyslexia Genetics' 2004

■ ■ ■

"My husband, the photographer/film director David Bailey, has dyspraxia. His work shows that he has not been hindered by it. His dyspraxia has forced him to view the world in a unique and original way."

Catherine Bailey (president of the Dyspraxia Foundation) 2000

■　■　■

What is dyslexia? There have been many attempts at defining it, but none is completely satisfactory. This is partly because we still do not know its exact cause, and partly because it manifests itself in a number of ways. It is perhaps best to see it as a cluster of characteristics, most of which dyslexics will experience, but not necessarily all of them. It is also the case that about half of dyslexics are dyspraxic (with bodily co-ordination difficulties) and many have dyscalculia (problems with numbers).

The latest research suggests that it is the interaction of a handful of genes, possibly on the short arm of chromosome 6, which causes dyslexia. Its key effect relates to phonological awareness – the ability to recognise the sounds which make up words – and also the speed of this language processing. So one of the main problems dyslexics have is connecting the sound to the symbol, the spoken word to the written word. This is why the most common way of detecting dyslexia has been through reading and writing.

There may be added problems if the sounds of the spoken word are 'non-standard' because of accent or dialect, as Cline and Reason point out in an article on equal opportunities issues: "It seems reasonable to suppose that children who are at risk of specific learning difficulties because of immature phonological awareness and memory will face heightened difficulties if the dialect or language they are accustomed to at home is different from the one adopted in school and in printed books."

This affects children with working-class accents and also those, for instance, who retain their Caribbean dialect. As Viv Edwards pointed out thirty years ago: "Many words which are quite distinct for the British are homonyms [words which sound the same] for West Indians." She gives as examples 'here' and 'hair', which are both pronounced 'here', and 'toy' and 'tie', both pronounced 'tie'.

Similarly many children learn more than one language in childhood, which may add to the phonological difficulties. In India, for example, pupils are expected to learn at least three languages, even at primary level.

READING AND WRITING

"Dyslexic children read and spell differently from normal readers qualitatively as well as quantitatively."

Elena Boder 'The Boder Test of Reading-Spelling Patterns' 1982

■ ■ ■

"The most pronounced among the reading difficulties that individuals with dyslexia experience is the inability to decode unfamiliar words. This problem appears to be the common denominator in all cases of dyslexia."

Joanna Kellogg Uhry & Diana Brewster Clark 'Dyslexia: Theory and Practice of Instruction' 2005

■ ■ ■

How do dyslexic children read? Often they get the clue from the shape of the word, rather than the sound of the letters. In fact most very young children probably recognise their first words like this. They may initially see their own name, for example, as a picture (logographic) rather than as a word. A child with a good visual memory may eventually store up quite a large collection of words in this way, to compensate for weak phonological skills. This is the basis of the 'look and say' method of teaching reading, where the word is usually anchored by being next to a picture.

When the image is missing, however, the word 'horse', for instance, may be read as 'house', because it is similar in shape. Hence "A horse divided against itself cannot stand!" What is needed to distinguish the two words is a grasp of phonics, to know how 'or' and 'ou' are pronounced in these words. If dyslexic readers are weak at analysing words phonetically, then they may simply look at the initial letter and guess at the word.

They may also omit or add words when reading a sentence. Sometimes they will substitute a word which **means** something similar, as well as words which **look** similar; for instance reading 'funny' instead of 'laugh', or 'answer' instead of 'ask'. In the end the reading may be an exercise in imaginative creation, rather than a reflection of what was written!

Little words, such as 'of', 'for' and 'from' are often confused and letters read back to front, like 'b' for 'd'; or upside down, 'm' instead of 'w'. Words

---

A horse divided against itself cannot stand.

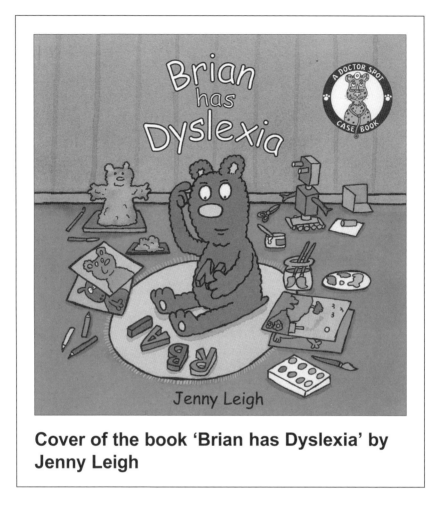

Cover of the book 'Brian has Dyslexia' by Jenny Leigh

are sometimes reversed: 'was' read as 'saw', 'dug' read as 'gud'; or they may be foreshortened, reading 'remember' as 'rember'.

Above all there may be no expression in the reading and no use of the punctuation to help in giving meaning to it. They may sometimes be able to read all the words fairly accurately, but the key question to ask is have they understood what they have been reading.

SPELLING

"'After all,' said Rabbit to himself, 'Christopher Robin depends on Me. He's fond of Pooh and Piglet and Eeyore, and so am I, but they haven't any Brain. Not to notice. And he respects Owl, because you can't help respecting anybody who can spell TUESDAY, even if he doesn't spell it right; but spelling isn't everything. There are days when spelling Tuesday simply doesn't count.'"

A. A. Milne 'The House at Pooh Corner' 1928

■ ■ ■

In the same way in which dyslexic reading follows particular patterns, so does the spelling. The one thing that most people know about dyslexic spelling is that the letters may be reversed, such as writing 'q' instead of 'p', or letters may be in the wrong sequence, as in the famous slogan 'Dyslexia Rules KO'.

Some of the typical errors are of this kind, writing 'de' for 'be', or 'babby' for 'daddy'. Sequencing difficulties can result in writing 'hlep' for 'help' or 'sonw' for 'snow'. Writing 'who' for 'how' can lead to a child sending a letter home:

Dear Mum,
Who are you and who is my dad?

Some omit letters: 'jup' instead of 'jump' or foreshorten the word: 'xprs' for 'express', 'amt' for 'amount'; some add letters: 'plan' for 'pan'. The shape may be similar, but the meaning completely different, for example spelling 'day' instead of 'dog' or 'flock' for 'float'. Sometimes duplication takes place, resulting in 'languaguage' or 'tokok' for 'talk'.

Some mistakes are clear attempts to spell phonetically, but come unstuck on the irregularities of English spelling: writing 'roowin' for 'ruin', 'blud' for 'blood', 'maget' for 'maggot' or 'coam' for 'comb'. Others seem to have little relationship to the sound of the word, for example spelling 'adventure' as 'aferch'. But even here, although '..ture' and '..ch' do not look alike, they do sound similar.

Spellings often seem completely bizarre until you realise what is happening in the mind of the speller. For instance, the word 'wusf' does not look

---

When a young dyslexic was asked to spell weather, she took a deep breath and plunged in, "w-h-e-r-e-t-h-e". The teacher regarded her with amazement and said, "That is certainly the worst spell of weather we've ever had."

like any English word. But if you see the 'w' as an upside down 'm' and the 'f' as a 't', then it is obviously 'must'. The logic and effort put into all these spelling mistakes should be recognised and not simply crossed out as wrong.

Sometimes 'l's are crossed and 't's not crossed, which gives you words spelt 'onty', 'slitt' and 'taler'. Occasionally words are split or joined inappropriately: 'yes terday', 'halfanhour'. The wrong letter may be doubled: 'eeg' for 'egg', 'beel' for 'bell'.

As with reading, many of these mistakes are made by non-dyslexic children, but with them they normally disappear at the age of 7 or 8. Within these patterns of dyslexic errors, it is important to

Drawing of Eeyore, Piglet, Rabbit, Pooh, Kanga, Roo and Owl

Cover of book by Jean Augur

analyse the kind of mistakes the students are making in order to decide what kind of help they need. Some are more to do with hearing the word (phonics), some more to do with writing it (orthography), and some involve both. If the difficulties are mainly to do with orthography, for example, the student may be far better at spelling orally than in written form.

SEQUENCING AND SHORT-TERM MEMORY

"For dyslexics, taking messages or remembering instructions are like holding a handful of fine sand. Dyslexics also have problems remembering dates, number strings, information and where they left their keys, laptop, gloves, watch, cigarettes, essay, coat and shoes. They rely on long-term memory, which is based more on association, context and understanding – all of which are dyslexic strengths."

Rosemary Scott 'Dyslexia and Counselling' 2004

■ ■ ■

But reading and writing alone do not define dyslexia. The consequences of being dyslexic are with you from the time you awake in the morning to the time you go to sleep at night. This is what non-dyslexics do not understand about dyslexia.

Weak sequencing skills and poor short-term memory affect dyslexics' ability to read and spell, but they also impinge on their everyday life. Sequencing is needed simply to put on your clothes and tie your shoes. It is necessary in order to remember the days of the week and months of the year, as well as the alphabet.

Eight-year-old girl's illustration of a policeman stopping the traffic

If a dyslexic child is told a list of shopping to buy, he or she may well have forgotten the first item by the time the last item is reached. If given a series of instructions to follow, the same thing will often happen. The order may be lost and also some of the individual instructions. Imagine how this might affect the work situation, as well as school.

At school great pressure is often put on dyslexic pupils when they are asked questions in class. They may not be able to process the language quickly enough and so will look as though they do not understand or are not paying attention. This leads to fear and avoidance tactics, even to being thrown out of the class or suspended.

Work can also present many dilemmas for the dyslexic, from applying for the job, to discovering where to go for the interview, to finding your way about on the first day. (This is why colour-coding in a building can be so helpful.) Then there is coping with the job: getting to work on time, deciding whether to 'come out' as a dyslexic or try and hide it, relating to colleagues, thinking what to do about promotion opportunities.

Time management is a problem. Dyslexics are often slow to learn to tell the time and weak at prioritising and completing tasks. Modern life is ruled by the clock and so many daily activities depend on organisational skills. Missing appointments, forgetting birthdays, losing keys, not

A dyslexic soldier was on an interrogation, information and escape course. He was given the information – the message. Then he escaped, was recaptured and interrogated. But he never broke down under interrogation because he forgot what the message was!

remembering names, confusing telephone numbers, remembering what to put in your bag - these can all be regular hazards for the dyslexic.

Dyslexics need more time to organise things and carry them out. Pressure to hurry up leads to stress and frustration, anger and despair. Yet modern life is based on speed and in many cultures, such as West Indian or Nigerian, for example, speed is a sign of intelligence. If you are slow, you must be stupid.

In British culture too, if you are quick, you must be clever. Think of all the quiz shows on television that demand speed of answer. 'Mastermind', for instance, has a time limit to answer the questions; 'Countdown' has a clock counting down the seconds; and in 'University Challenge' Jeremy Paxman keeps telling the students to hurry up and even gets faster in posing the questions, the nearer he gets to the end of the programme! The ultimate absurdity of this way of thinking is the exam, where you have to write down what you know, or can remember, in two hours, or two and a half hours, if you are dyslexic!

Two of the most common dyslexic mistakes are made when writing cheques and dialling telephone numbers, both of which rely on sequencing and short-term memory. The amount in words on the cheque often fails to agree with the amount in figures. Another area of difficulty is following a recipe in a cookery book, as this relies on reading, sequencing, timing, and measuring amounts. It also involves doing more than one thing at a time and this can cause problems.

In the same way, dyslexic students find it hard to listen to a lecture and also take notes, to copy from the board, and to look up words in an index or dictionary. They may be easily distracted too, by people talking or other noise interference. This can cause anxiety, stress and even panic. The extra concentration can lead to tiredness and frustration.

This also points to the fact that dyslexic students are regularly working many times harder than non-dyslexic students, which is ironic when you consider that they are often called lazy! In 'Dyslexia and Stress' Tim Miles estimates that whereas a non-dyslexic might take 100 hours to learn a skill, a dyslexic could take 1,000 hours.

Similarly an interdisciplinary team of University of Washington researchers claimed (in the American Journal of Neuroradiology, October 1999) that dyslexics used "4.6 times as much of the brain to do the same language task" as non-dyslexics. The neurophysicist Todd Richards goes

---

How do you hire a horse?

Put it on stilts.

Signs made by Jean Augur's son, Chris, for a library scene in a play

on to say: "This means their brains were working a lot harder and using more energy than the normal children." Virginia Berninger, a professor of educational psychology, adds: "People often don't see how hard it is for dyslexic children to do a task that others do so effortlessly."

Sequencing may be even more crucial in relation to the law. If you cannot remember times and dates and the sequence of events when confronted by the police or a judge, then the consequences can be severe. Dyslexics have been known to be overloud and rambling when arrested, and inconsequential as if trying to avoid the question. In 'Dyslexia and the Law' Melanie Jameson describes a dyslexic who was "unable to express himself without striding about the room, using his whole body in an attempt to help the words out". (Of course this is also a cultural issue, as some cultures, such as Caribbean or Italian, for example, use far more gestures and body language than others.)

99

'The Times' of January 1998 described Richard Branson in court during a libel case as "um-ing and ah-ing, wrestling to remember events and dates and drying up completely at one stage. He could only stutter 'I'm sorry, my mind's gone blank... what on earth... I can't remember what the, what do you mean?'" Afterwards he said: "As a family we often just can't get our words out."

In 'Reversals: A Personal Account of Victory over Dyslexia', Eileen Simpson describes this sense of confusion: "It did not surprise me to learn that the seat of the disorder is in the brain. In my own case I had localized it there at age nine. (I had felt, or believed I had felt, a brainache, which is quite different from a headache.) The jamming, blocking, and confusion I suffered from I had likened to a mechanical breakdown – an out-of-order switchboard, two typewriter keys locking so that neither prints."

Finished by Gemma Varciana

I never finish anything.

Everything I say, I stop in between, get distracted and then forget what I am going to say

When I was at school I remembered…

I never finish anything.

"You will never amount to anything" they'll say
"You always get distracted and you'd probably forget everything I've just said" Mum always said…

I never finish anything.

Teachers would say that I get distracted too easily and mum said that she would never give me anything to do because I would forget in the middle of it and stop.

I never finish anything.

But I remembered everything they said and I've just finished this poem!

CIRCUMLOCUTION

"Sterne didn't want unity or coherence or defined direction, at least in any conventional sense; he wanted multiplicity, not unity; he wanted free association of ideas, not subordination of them; he wanted to go backwards or forwards or sideways, not in straight linear paths."

Ian Watt 'The Comic Syntax of 'Tristram Shandy" 1967

■ ■ ■

"By indirections find directions out."

William Shakespeare 'Hamlet' 1600

■ ■ ■

"The person who thinks in a linear manner often misses the important resemblances of the concepts contained within subjects that are separated by the artificial subject boundaries, such as Chemistry, Biology, Physics, Electronics, Art etc."

Stephen Summerfield 'A Social and Educational Case-History of Dyslexia' 1993

■ ■ ■

"Progress is not in a straight line."

C.L.R. James 'Modern Politics' 1960

■ ■ ■

Circumlocution ('circum' – round, 'locution' – speaking) is a long word to describe a long process, namely going all round the houses to get to the point, or never actually getting to the point! The vagueness and inaccuracy involved can be very frustrating for someone who is more sequentially organised in their thought processes, but in the appropriate context circumlocution can be both entertaining and enlightening.

The celebrated eighteenth-century novel 'Tristram Shandy' by the Irish writer Laurence Sterne is 600 pages of circumlocution. It is a long shaggy dog story, a joke whose point is that there is no point. On the last page he calls it a cock and bull story. It progresses by digressing, as the author explains: "In a word, my work is digressive, and it is progressive too, - and at the same time." It's like life itself: the point is to live it, not just get to the end!

It is significant that Sterne was Irish, for Irish culture, like West Indian culture, is famous for its entertaining story-telling. Similarly the West African griots are masters in the art of circumlocution,

Laurence Sterne

never going straight to the point. The main interest in their stories is supposed to be in the incidental episode, not in the climax. Perhaps it is partly a response to the conquering linearity of the English, a way of confusing them and putting them off the scent, a reply to the pointed brutality of the sign that used to go up, saying 'No dogs, no blacks, no Irish'.

In English culture too there is a subversive tradition of elaborate story-telling which challenges authority. It is well represented in Shakespeare, from Falstaff's imaginative inventions to the digressions of the Fool in 'King Lear'. The Fool goes off at tangents all the time and manages in this way to call King Lear a fool. The Fool himself is in fact the wisest character in the play.

Many dyslexics succeed in the story-telling business, as actors, comedians or performance poets. Then it becomes an advantage to "stride about and use your whole body"! It is also the case that, although the short-term memory may be weak, the dyslexic's long-term memory may be very strong. As the actress Beryl Reid said: "Dyslexia has been a very good part of my life because I never forget anything. Once I have learnt something, I can't forget it."

What did the judge say when the skunk came into the court room?

"Odour in the court."

ORIENTATION

"Map-reading, filling out forms, reading aloud, reading road signs are just a few of a long list of things that I find really frustrating. However, with good luck and a great deal of hard work I have managed to master my job."

Susan Hampshire 'Dyslexia and Stress' 1995

■   ■   ■

Sequencing is about order in time; orientation is about order in space. Just as our day is governed by time, our movement depends on concepts of space. Although dyslexics may be skilled at finding their way around by experience and visual clues, they rarely find it easy to read a map. Matching the symbolic representation to the physical reality is hard.

The points of the compass can present difficulties too, especially as north and south, for example, can change depending on where you are. Similarly left and right are often confused, for again they are reversed for someone who is facing you. It is no use labelling shoes left and right if a child cannot tell the difference, though marking the **outside** of each shoe may well help.

These difficulties will make driving and following directions hard. They will also affect school subjects such as geography and physical education.

Driving a car illustrates another aspect of a dyslexic's problems. It involves automaticity, which means the way some activities become automatic. For instance, changing gear without looking, whilst listening to the sound of the engine, soon becomes automatic to non-dyslexics. But dyslexics need to concentrate consciously on these simultaneous actions for a lot longer. This is the same issue which affects reading and spelling – the failure of certain routine skills to become automatic.

How many ants are needed to fill an apartment?

Ten-ants.

VISUAL THINKING

"I think in pictures. Words are like a second language to me. I translate both spoken and written words into full-color movies, complete with sound, which runs like a VCR tape in my head. When somebody speaks to me, his words are instantly translated into pictures. Language-based thinkers often find this phenomenon difficult to understand, but in my job as an equipment designer for the livestock industry, visual thinking is a tremendous advantage."

Temple Grandin 'Thinking in Pictures: and Other Reports from My Life with Autism' 1996

■ ■ ■

"Some dyslexic people, myself included, do appear to develop a form of autism and this has a great impact on perception and sensuality. I would go so far as to argue that it is not the mind of the dyslexic that knows this or that, but rather the rhythm of his or her body."

Christine Kenny 'Living and Learning with Dyslexia: The Medusa's Gaze' 2002

■ ■ ■

"Perhaps institutions with enough imagination to see the potential value of innovative, visual-thinking dyslexics may have enough imagination to anticipate and outwit future threats. If some neurologists are correct, this is the role that strong visual thinkers and dyslexics have played for many thousands of years: having different brains and different perspectives – to allow individuals and groups to see unexpected patterns, to see what is coming over the horizon, to see what others do not see."

Thomas G. West 'Thinking Like Einstein' 2004

■ ■ ■

Dyslexics can improve their language processing and learn to use compensatory strategies, but the issue still persists. The neurons in the brain learn different pathways, but the original blockage remains. But all is not lost. A detour may take longer, but the scenery may be much more beautiful!

It certainly seems that dyslexia, like autism, produces visual thinkers. The autistic designer Temple Grandin explains how the educational system works against such thinkers: "During my career, I have met many brilliant visual thinkers in the maintenance departments of meat plants.

Some of these people are great designers and invent all kinds of innovative equipment, but they were disillusioned and frustrated at school. Our educational system weeds these people out of the system instead of turning them into world-class scientists."

This is also the view of Elizabeth Fleming, who is dyslexic, along with all five of her children. In 'Believe the Heart: Our Dyslexic Days', she writes: "Dyslexics think in concepts and pictures instead of words. Until very recently, I didn't know that anyone thought in words. Can you imagine the problems that arise when an educator or parent who thinks in words tries to teach a child who thinks in pictures and concepts?"

The autistic artist Stephen Wiltshire was mute as a child and expressed himself by drawing. He could look at a building briefly and then draw it accurately from memory. With the support of his mother and sister, and the staff at Queensmill Primary School in west London, he learnt to talk and read and write, and decided he wanted to be an architect. He eventually travelled the world and produced four books of his drawings and paintings.

Why is the theatre a sad place?

Because the seats are always in tiers.

Stephen Wiltshire

When visual thinking is encouraged and developed, it can lead on to great things, as we have seen also with Leonardo da Vinci and Einstein. Visual-spatial skills are needed in so many spheres of activity, such as art and design, engineering, architecture, computer graphics, sport. If you can think in 3D, see the whole picture from different angles, make unexpected connections, you are at an advantage.

In 'Thinking Like Einstein', Thomas G. West, who learnt he was dyslexic at the age of 41, writes: "I believe we are now at the early stages of a major transition – moving from an old world of

Drawing of Tower Bridge by Stephen Wiltshire, aged nine

education and work largely based on words and numbers to a new world largely based on images that are rich in content and information."

He quotes an American cryptographer, Roy Follendore, who said "every research and investigation team should have at least one dyslexic on it". West adds: "This bold (and improbable) measure could ensure that the group would not get stuck in some eddy of thought and not be able to move forward – or alternatively, would avoid the group moving forward in the wrong direction."

West also sees the importance of visual thinking in education: "If a picture is worth a thousand words, some say a moving computer visualization in 3D is worth a million words. For example, one short video visualization about the possibility of planets orbiting round a distant pulsar is said to compress 12 to 15 hours of conventional university lectures into just three minutes."

Five hundred years ago Leonardo was saying the same thing. Referring to his anatomical drawings which he made for his own research, he wrote: "No one could hope to convey so much true knowledge without an immense, tedious and confused length of writing and time, except through this very short way of drawing from different aspects."

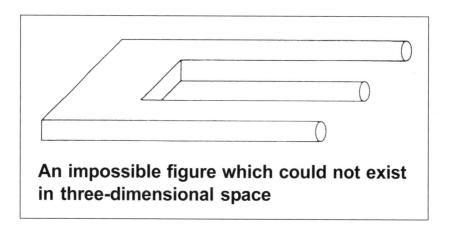

An impossible figure which could not exist in three-dimensional space

A recent study, published in 2004, indicates that "dyslexia is linked with a specific talent in global visual spatial abilities". The researchers, von Karoly and Winner, discovered that dyslexics were faster and more accurate at identifying impossible figures, which could not exist in three-dimensional space, such as Escher's drawings. This suggests, they conclude, that "dyslexia is accompanied by a very specific kind of visual-spatial talent – rapid and accurate holistic inspection".

From 'Dyslexia: Talking it Through' by Althea Braithwaite & Frances Cony

On the other hand, Qona Rankin, from the Royal College of Art, sounds a note of caution. In 'Dyslexia Art and Design' she recounts how some of her dyslexic students find certain types of drawing difficult, particularly those involving orientation and short-term memory. There is clearly a danger of assuming that all dyslexics are artistically talented.

Dyslexia does often seem to be accompanied by both literal and lateral thinking. "Thou shalt not kill" appears to be straightforward and not to be confused with "Thou shalt not kill thy neighbour, but thou canst kill as many Iraqis as thou wouldst like." In the same way, lateral or divergent thinking is often a dyslexic strength – seeing alternatives and the big picture, rather than just the details. Perhaps as well as having a dyslexic in every research team, there should be more dyslexics in the United Nations!

DYSLEXISMS AND HUMOUR

"Many a dyslexic gets by through becoming the classroom clown."

Macdonald Critchley 1980

■ ■ ■

"Dyslexics hate to be laughed at."

Jean Augur 1981

■ ■ ■

"I found that by playing the clown it got me through some of the fears I had at school and at home."

Bob Turney 1997

■ ■ ■

"Arbolist... Look up the word. I don't know, maybe I made it up. Anyway, it's an arbo-tree-ist, somebody who knows about trees."

George W. Bush 2001

■ ■ ■

116

"The class clown at school is a very common dyslexic school role."

Rosemary Scott 2004

■ ■ ■

In her autobiography 'Reversals: A Personal Account of Victory over Dyslexia', Eileen Simpson records how she became popular as the 'class clown'. She explains that she used to pretend that her slips of the tongue were intentional. These verbal slips are a hallmark of dyslexia, so could well be called dyslexisms. They include Freudian slips, malapropisms and spoonerisms.

While dyslexics may turn these errors to their advantage, they may find some kinds of verbal humour difficult to understand. The pun, for example, depends on grasping the fact that two

In the Oval Office George Bush is being briefed by Rumsfeld on the Iraq War. Rumsfeld says: "I have to tell you, Mr President, that yesterday three Brazilian soldiers were killed." To his surprise Bush groans and buries his head in his hands, saying over and over, "That's just terrible, terrible news. Remind me again, just how many is a brazillion?"

words sound the same but have different meanings (homophone), such as 'sole' and 'soul', or that two words which are spelt the same mean two different things (homonym), like 'Pole' and 'pole'. So getting the joke can depend on spelling and phonics, but also on the sequencing and short-term memory needed to go back and forth between the two meanings.

This may make Shakespeare's 'Love's Labours Lost', for example, difficult to follow, as it contains over 200 puns. In all Shakespeare's plays there are over a thousand puns – 1,062 to be precise! Falstaff alone utters 59.

The pun is a conscious play on words, whereas the malapropism is unconscious. The term comes from the character of Mrs Malaprop in 'The Rivals' (1775), a comedy by the Irish playwright Richard Brinsley Sheridan. She gets her name from the French phrase meaning

Richard Brinsley Sheridan

Bottom, from Shakespeare's 'A Midsummer Night's Dream'

inappropriate, as for instance when she says: "He is as headstrong as an allegory on the banks of the Nile." She is a figure of fun because she is pretentious, whilst making obvious mistakes.

Shakespeare invented a number of characters who made similar errors. They are nearly all working-class people, such as Bottom in 'A Midsummer's Night Dream', or Launcelot Gobbo in 'The Merchant of Venice', who are laughed at for their mistakes. The most well-known is Dogberry in 'Much Ado About Nothing', who says, for example: "You are thought here to be the most senseless and fit man for the constable of the watch; therefore bear you the lantern." His most famous phrase is "Comparisons are odorous."

BRING THE DYSLEXIC BACK ON
by Asher Hoyles

I want to say you look exotic
But I'll probably say you look erotic
I'd like to say you're situated
But I may say you're saturated

Exotic
Erotic
Situated
Saturated

I want to call the whole thing
Should I call the whole thing
Want to call the whole thing off

Because I'll see pursued
And you'll say persuaded
I'll read maintained
And you'll say marinated
Because maintained and marinated
Well that would change the meaning

I want to call the whole thing
Should I call the whole thing
Want to call the whole thing off

But oh….
If only I knew my phonics
I'd have a tactic
And oh if only I could really grasp it
Man I would practise…

Ah, buh, cuh, duh, eh, fuh
Guh, huh, ih, juh, kuh, luh
Muh, nuh, oh, puh, quh, ruh
Suh, tuh, uh, vuh, wuh
X, yuh
X, yuh
Z
Z
Z
Z
Z

Then I wouldn't say you're eccentric
When I really mean you're electric
And I wouldn't say you've been relegated
When I mean I'm just regulating

Because I've got myself some phonics
Found myself a tactic
Witness how I practise
So bring the dyslexic back on

abcdef (recited phonetically as above)
ghijkl
mnopqr
stuvw
xy
xy
z
z
z
z.....

SPOONERISMS

"Spooner's slips were not normal errors, and were probably due to a motor disability, caused by developmental dyslexia."

Victoria A. Fromkin 1980

■ ■ ■

"Spoonerisms are the relatives of the portmanteau words of Lewis Carroll, of the sayings of Mrs Malaprop, and of rhyming slang. All these can be employed imaginatively, even creatively, as Joyce used puns with such brilliance in 'Finnegans Wake'."

John M. Potter 1980

■ ■ ■

The spoonerism is a very important dyslexism. It involves swapping round the first letters of words, such as 'par cark' or 'beg and acorn'. Dyslexics may do it unconsciously, but significantly find it hard to do consciously. This is why the task of exchanging initial letters is useful in assessing dyslexia. It is difficult because, as with the pun, it involves spelling, phonics, sequencing and short-term memory.

William Archibald Spooner

Similarly, sounding out nonsense words is usually difficult, especially in English with its irregular spelling. German dyslexic children find it easier, but are still very slow at reading non-words.

Lewis Carroll's poem 'Jabberwocky' is a good example of inventing new words:

'Twas brillig, and the slithy toves
    Did gyre and gimble in the wabe:
All mimsy were the borogoves,
    And the mome raths outgrabe.

William Archibald Spooner (1844-1930) was warden of New College, Oxford, where he was a lecturer and dean. He is famous for sayings such as "Our Lord is a shoving leopard", and "I only know two tunes – 'God Save the Weasel' and 'Pop Goes the Queen'." He is said to have told a student: "You have tasted a whole worm and you have hissed my mystery lectures." Going into church he said, "Is this pie occupewed?" Many of these spoonerisms were probably invented by students and other people. One is about a farmer's wife in Tibet who smelled something burning and rushed out to the barn moaning, "Oh, my baking yak!"

But Dr Spooner did certainly get people's names mixed up, calling Mr Russell Brain - Mr Brain Russell, and saying Dr Friend's child instead of Dr Childe's friend. He also once asked a friend: "Was it you or your brother who was killed in the war?"

His sequencing problems extended to his actions, as when he accidentally spilled some salt on the tablecloth and then poured some wine on it,

"Let me sew you to your sheet," said the usher.

Illustration from 'Runny Babbit' by Shel Silverstein

drop by drop, in order to remove it. He once also remarked on the darkness of a staircase before turning off the one light which was on and attempting to lead a party of guests down the stairs.

His speech was often slow and hesitant as if he was choosing his words with care, but then there would be sudden bursts of speed. He also made odd slips of the pen as if his mind ran ahead of his hand. Sometimes he was ridiculed for his short-sightedness and for being an albino, but he certainly got the last laugh on his students. At his final college dinner the undergraduates called for a speech. Spooner made a perfect and charming speech and then, at the end, said: "And now I suppose you will expect me to say one of **those things**, but I shan't!" And he sat down.

In his article 'What Was the Matter with Dr Spooner', John M. Potter concludes: "It seems possible to me that Spooner's trouble might be regarded as an essentially motor member of that family of developmental disorders which has developmental dyslexia as its outstanding example."

TIGGER

"Bouncing and mispronouncing are what Tiggers do best."

Tigger

■ ■ ■

Tigger is both dyspraxic and dyslexic. In 'The House at Pooh Corner' A. A. Milne writes: "Tigger accidentally knocked over one or two chairs by accident." Tigger also utters a few dyslexisms,

Tigger, from A.A. Milne's 'The House at Pooh Corner'

such as "Tiggers don't like haycorns" and "They're very good flyers, Tiggers are. Strornry [extraordinary] good flyers."

But it is in the cartoon versions on television where he really comes into his own. From being a minor character in the book, he becomes major on the screen, carrying the show with his bounce and long words, invented or misapplied. "Wait a minuet", he says, "you've got to have the right

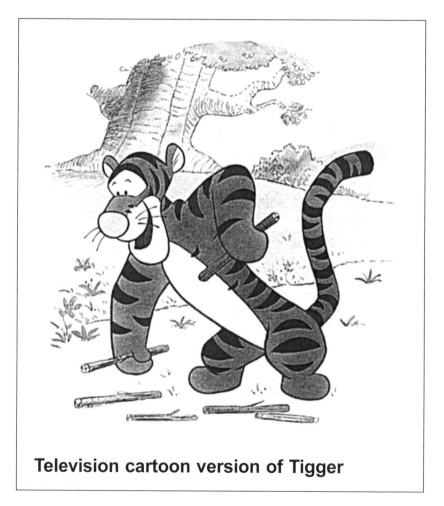

Television cartoon version of Tigger

mental altitude." He talks about "Spanish spittoons" (doubloons) in the treasure they are looking for, and "X spots the mark!"

He confuses words: perspiring/inspiring, illumination/elimination, continent/consonant; and invents words: dinosnores, exaggertated. He also produces an example of what Lewis Carroll called portmanteau words: hilarical (a combination of hilarious and hysterical). Even when saying goodbye, he gets his rhyme wrong: "See you later, crocodile!"

Humour is expressed in all cultures, though often in different ways. It is a social interaction and to be left out can be cruel. We like laughing, but we do not like being laughed at. If dyslexics have been labelled slow and stupid, it is not surprising that they do not like being laughed at for not getting jokes. The trick is to be laughed **with**, and you only have to look at comedians like Whoopi Goldberg and Angie Le Mar to see how successful dyslexics can be.

Laughter is infectious and it may be because of dyslexics' literal and lateral thinking that they can often bring hilarity to a situation, where non-dyslexics are being so serious.

ANGER

"Knowledge can be a dangerous thing. I now believe that there are very good neurological reasons for my failing to be 'normal'. I feel a tremendous anger and bitterness towards the people who have unjustly hurt me: family, friends, teachers, classmates, etc."

Alison Hale 'My World is not Your World' 1998

"I had a great deal of pent-up anger as a result of my dyslexia and I often wound up in fights in the school playground. Fortunately, I found an outlet for my energy – I became an excellent runner and channelled my anger into a positive activity."

Robert Frank 'The Secret Life of the Dyslexic Child' 2003

It is sometimes a short road between humour and rage, especially if the humour has been directed at you. Frustration and anger are often part of the dyslexic's experience.

Stephen Summerfield took part in an active dyslexic self-help group during his last year of research for his PhD in Chemistry at Loughborough University of Technology. He describes the process, both physical and mental, of becoming furious: "I still know what it is to have the dyslexic's blind fury when I cannot

How do you kill a circus?

Go straight for the juggler.

comprehend or be comprehended. The stages in the build up of fury are:

a) Severe agitation.
b) A fixed stare like a scared animal caught in the lights of a speeding car and the brooding silence before the storm.
c) My muscles in arms tense and my fists clench. The tension causes shaking in the rest of the body.

Why did the chicken get sent off?

For persistent fowl play.

d) I then feel like running away and hiding. This is expressed by me either just walking away, hiding behind clenched fists shaking visibly or destroying some poor inanimate, including picking to pieces a rubber, throwing keys at the laboratory door, punching a hole in a partition wall or screwing up the essays that I had to iron flat later.

e) My fury and temper would be under the surface and would then be sparked off for no apparent reason by anything or anybody. It would often take me days to calm down.

This blind fury has been controlled but not eliminated. Many of my close friends recognize the signals and stay out of my way."

This kind of experience is ignored in most of the literature on dyslexia, as Summerfield points out: "Nobody understands until they have lived through it, and especially those so-called specialists who should know better." But he ends on a more light-hearted note: "My ear-piercing laughter has been described as like a strangled cat. Many people have said that they do not look for me in a crowd but listen to where the noise is coming from."

Again it must be stressed that not all dyslexics will experience all of these things. But most will experience most of them to some extent.

SELF-ESTEEM

"About a third of my students are dyslexic. Many have 'successfully' evaded detection throughout their education and are statemented while on this course. All these students have suffered loss of self-esteem, lack of value in their abilities and have a variety of difficulties associated not with dyslexia, but with their experience as a result of being dyslexic."

Morag Kiziewicz (special needs coordinator and lecturer at the University of the West of England) 1999

■ ■ ■

"The educational system in Egypt depends mostly on the written word, and the Egyptian educational system still regards mis-spelling and poor reading ability as directly related to stupidity and a low level of intelligence."

'International Book of Dyslexia' 2004

■ ■ ■

"If you don't have a word for it, like dyslexia, you really do believe you're dumb. I was dumb because I was Black. I was dumb because I couldn't read and write. This is what I was telling myself."

Benjamin Zephaniah 'The Mystery of the Lost Letters' BBC 2004

■ ■ ■

If you are told often enough that you are stupid, it is likely that you will believe it. One of the main tasks of the dyslexic is to overcome this belief. A long-term visual memory can be a disadvantage, because it means you can actually feel again the bullying, teasing and ridicule that you experienced as a child, particularly at school, and which often continues into adulthood. This is why it is so useful for dyslexics to come together as a group to share their experiences.

Bob Turney left school at fifteen years of age, unable to read and write and hardly able to sign his name. He became a drug addict and spent eighteen years drifting in and out of prison. In his autobiography 'I'm Still Standing' he describes how he finally realised he was dyslexic: "People thought that I was stupid or lazy, or just not interested. However, children of all abilities can have dyslexia. My self-esteem plummeted until it was almost non-existent. It was not until I was in my late forties that I started to believe in myself and stopped thinking I was a fool, and it has taken me a long time with a lot of help from my wife, children and friends to rid myself of the belief that I was some kind of imbecile."

Most cultures look down on disabled people. They have been blamed for their disability, looked on as cursed by God, or at best pitied. In England a dyslexic can be called a dummy; in Nigeria the Yoruba word used is 'olodo', meaning you are a fool and know nothing; in China the word for disabled is 'canfei' (pronounced tsan-fay) which also means useless or worthless.

Emma Stone explains how the Chinese Government has introduced a new word 'canji' (tsan-jee), which is a neutral word for people with impairments. They have also invented a new slogan 'canji erbu canfei', meaning 'disabled but not useless'.

In Beijing she interviewed a disabled artist and activist called Mr Liu, who told her: "There are so many differences with the past. Before the 1980s, all the newspapers and broadcasts would call us 'canfei' people. The word itself tells you so much! Under appeal from many disabled people, newspapers and the rest of the media changed and started using 'canji' people. Since then, step by step, the rest of society has started to change."

It is a slow process, but hopefully this book will make a contribution. The interviews which follow reveal major achievements of Black dyslexics in modern British society. As explained in the introduction, Black people are missing from the dyslexic scene, just as they were written out of history until very recently. There is a major gap in the literature, which needs to be filled.

In a recent book 'Dyslexia: A Practical Guide for Teachers and Parents' (2002), for example, 14 famous dyslexics are mentioned, all of them white,

Camels are mainly found in the dessert.

and this in a chapter entitled Raising Self-esteem! There are over 700 books on dyslexia in the British Library, but apparently not one by a Black writer, and none of them deals with the issue of race or ethnicity.

This situation is unlikely to make dyslexia a burning topic of conversation in the Black communities, nor bring any enlightenment and encouragement to Black dyslexics who need support. We fervently hope that this book will open up the subject for debate and discussion, and lead to improved awareness amongst all people in our society.

INTERVIEWS

CAROLE MILES

Carole Miles was born on 19 April 1963, in Stockwell, South London. She first found out she was dyslexic in 1998. She now has a BSc in Anthropology from the University of East London and an MA in Television Documentaries from Goldsmith's College. She is also a qualified counsellor specialising in dyslexic adults (info@dyslexia-care.com).

From a young age she believed she was stupid and was regularly humiliated about it, as she recalls: "One of my earliest memories of school is asking the teacher a question, but she didn't know the answer. So I thought, what am I doing, I'm stupid, don't ask. I became totally withdrawn. I was a nervous wreck at school."

Her dyslexia showed itself in her spelling which was "terrible" and her reading: "When I left school I couldn't read. I had to tutor myself. I remember living in a squat in Hackney, thinking I've got to do something about it. I got really fed up, so I started looking at books and trying to figure out how to read. Then I remember reading my first book from cover to cover. It was 'Jonathan

Carole Miles

Livingston Seagull' by Richard Bach, about a gull and his journey of self-discovery, so it really mirrored my own journey."

When she first went to school, she stopped eating for about 3 months: "I was traumatised. When I was about 7, the teacher called me up to the front of the class and told me to read. I couldn't read, everything became a blur and I froze. So the teacher grabbed the book, read out a sentence and then told me again to read it. I still couldn't, so she slapped me across the face. I think it wasn't just because of the reading, but also because I was Black. I just sat there dazed and the next thing I knew, the class was empty and the cleaner was calling me and I went home. I was just horrified."

Carole's parents are Jamaican, who owned land up in the mountains of Portland. They are descended from Maroons, escaped slaves who lived an independent life in the interior of the island. Her cultural background is reflected in a story she tells about her father: "He told me once to go to the doctor's and get a 'surfer ticket'. I went and asked for it, but was told they hadn't got any, so I went back and told my dad. Then my mum came to the rescue and said that he meant a 'certificate'!"

> **"I became totally withdrawn. I was a nervous wreck at school."**

> **"I was trying to get some basic adult literacy going and I went, year in, year out, and every time I went I was treated like a complete idiot."**

Another time she was on a bus with her mum, trying to read a 'No Smoking' sign: "I broke it up and said something like 'Nosmo King'. I remember two white ladies looking at me and mumbling something. My mum was totally humiliated, and she still never actually told me what it said."

As an adult, Carole continually went to try and register for classes to find some help with her reading and writing: "It took me a long time to have the nerve to go into a school building. They scared me so much. Well into my adult years I was still terrified. I thought I have to go and walk into this building which held so much trauma for me. I was trying to get some basic adult literacy going and I went, year in, year out, and every time I went I was treated like a complete idiot."

She recalls one typical experience: "One time I walked into a class where everyone was already sitting and the teacher said to me, 'Carole, next week you need to bring an exercise book.' So I said all right and she said, 'Do you know what an exercise book is?' I said yes and she said, 'Serena, show Carole the exercise book.' I was already earning twice as much as her and had a successful career in the media. I still ended up getting treated like an idiot, so I didn't go back."

Carole persevered, however, and went one last time to a college: "I was asked by the English teacher to do some tests to see what level I was at. He looked at my writing and said he thought I was dyslexic. I didn't know what that meant, but he asked me to do a further basic assessment and said he really thought I was dyslexic."

When she went to university she was properly assessed and found out she was dyslexic: "I was devastated, realising that there was something wrong with me, that there was some part of me that didn't actually work properly. I took it that way. It was really most upsetting and depressing. At the time there was no support around. I was told and then told to get on with it. For about 4 weeks I spiralled inwards feeling I was broken. I was broken and couldn't be fixed. The whole process led me to re-examine my whole life in the light of that information. I had to re-shuffle my memories of my life, so initially it was a terrible devastation and shock, but eventually it turned around."

> **"My dad asked me if I was going to a real university. He couldn't believe it, but I was so pleased when he came to my graduation. He was so proud."**

> **"I am totally pro-dyslexia. I would never ever wish my dyslexia away."**

Carole felt that she could not go back to university because she felt so ashamed: "I was struggling, but just about managing. I saw one of my tutors and said I had to leave. He said why and I said because everyone will know. He said that people don't need to know. I went to the students' union and saw a counsellor. That helped enormously, just to get over that initial shock."

She also contacted ADO (Adult Dyslexia Organisation) and phoned Donald Schloss: "He had a long conversation with me and said that I had done the first semester, so why couldn't I do the second one too! He eventually convinced me and I went back. He was so helpful that day and if it wasn't for him I don't think I would have gone back to university. My dad asked me if I was going to a real university. He couldn't believe it, but I was so pleased when he came to my graduation. He was so proud."

At work in the media, Carole usually avoids having to write things and manages to read enough to get by, as long as she is not frightened: "If I'm frightened, I can't even see the page. I remember once at work, someone said, 'I'm going to show you how to do so-and-so.' I just went white-blind with terror that I was going to be exposed, with the shame of it all. Your personality is wrapped up with what you can't do, not what you can do. You're terrified that people will find out and they will reject you. It's quite merciless. My experience of West Indian families is that they don't mince words. They will call you an idiot. I remember when I was about nine, a neighbour who was West Indian, came up to me and said, 'You're a cabbage.'"

She admits that her time-keeping was awful and she would turn up late everywhere: "My employers would keep giving me warnings and say, 'If you come in late one more time I'm going to sack you!' But now I understand my dyslexia, I am able to manage my time-keeping."

Carole thinks there are strengths in dyslexics, for example global thinking and linking theory with actuality. She believes the issue of dyslexia should be raised more often in the West Indian community and concludes: "I am totally pro-dyslexia. I would never ever wish my dyslexia away. It's an amazing gift. It's a part of me and I love that part of me now."

TAIWO AKINOLA

Taiwo was born in Nigeria in 1959. When he started primary school he knew there was a problem, but did not know what it was: "I found dates difficult. Even knowing the difference between Monday and Tuesday, or remembering how many days there are in a week, or months in a year, was hard. Telling the time was difficult. Even now I find it hard to work out the twenty-four hour clock. Multiplication tables and spelling I found very difficult, especially when I compared myself to my half-sister who was in the same class as me. Teachers used to say that I had the ability, if only I could concentrate. It wasn't until I came to the UK for my university education that I was able to realise what it was."

Discovering that he was dyslexic came to Taiwo quite by accident: "I was reading 'The Guardian' on the tube and there was a reference to dyslexia, identifying ten of its main characteristics. So when I read the ten, I realised that at least nine and a half applied to me! Then I knew that I was dyslexic. I contacted the telephone number in the article and started to read more about it, though it took another two or three years before I decided to have some treatment."

Taiwo was a hundred per cent sure he was dyslexic and realised it was ongoing: "It wasn't just the experience of childhood and then it was gone. It was still there. In my day-to-day life I experienced it. I could see the gap between my intellect and the problem I had with communicating, especially writing. This has stayed with me till this moment. It has made it difficult to make the best use of my intellectual abilities, even though I now have a Diploma in Management, an MA in Diplomatic Studies and an MSc in Transport Management. But the intuitive gift derived from it is also priceless."

At home in Nigeria, he remembers a positive side to his dyslexia: "When I came home from school, I was able to tell my parents what had happened at home while I was away, and I remember a few occasions when my mother would ask me how I noticed. Out of the blue you are able to discover things. This intuition started at the age of five or six and made me feel very happy. The negative side was that my school work was weak. I was a very active child and I was always being told that I wasn't concentrating. It is true that we

---

"I was reading 'The Guardian' on the tube and there was a reference to dyslexia, identifying ten of its main characteristics. I realised that at least nine and a half applied to me!"

Taiwo Akinola

have a restless and inquisitive mind. On the one hand there was this cleverness that I was capable of at home, but it didn't match with how I performed at school."

"In Nigeria there are millions of dyslexics who unfortunately do not know what the problem is and are probably made to believe that they are slow learners, when in terms of intellectual ability, they could be among the most gifted in the world. Their talents are being wasted and their lives ruined just because they don't know how good they are. They are unable to separate the gift from the problem and then make maximum use of it. They are being made to believe that they are not academically bright and then many of them drop out of school."

At work, in the office, most people don't know he has a problem: "Even when I say that I have a problem, people often don't believe me because they think I'm smart enough and know this and that, but they are not aware that I am unable to operate to the best of my abilities. Sometimes people notice my difficulties and either think I am not interested in what I am doing, or just

"On the one hand there was this cleverness that I was capable of at home, but it didn't match with how I performed at school."

> **"It's like water running through a tunnel and all of a sudden the volume of water is more than the tunnel can take and you suffer from disorientation."**

pretending not to be able to do it. The simplest things become very, very difficult. It's like water running through a tunnel and all of a sudden the volume of water is more that the tunnel can take and you suffer from disorientation. It's like you're driving and you're not sure whether things are moving backward or forward. You lose total concentration."

Finding the way and following instructions can also be hard: "When I ask the way in the street, as soon as the first bit of information is given me, I've forgotten it. I have to remember not to panic, but to calm down. In the past I would just be unsure of what to do. Now, if I'm driving, I just park and then look for a better way. It doesn't solve the problem, but it's a way to deal with it. I never drive in the dark because I know I'll get lost."

People make judgements on dyslexics based on very limited information: "Sometimes, being dyslexic, you find it easier to crack difficult problems than basic ones. For instance, simple spellings that your children could do, like 'grammar' or 'international', or distinguishing between 'sleep' and 'slip'. People then judge you on that and think that's a reflection of your intellectual ability. It's very frustrating!"

Writing presents problems for Taiwo: "I put off writing things for weeks, just because I don't want to face it. I read the newspapers and feel like replying to so many things, where I know the relevant concepts, but unless it's absolutely necessary, I won't do it. Dyslexics have difficulty with phonics and if you can't sound the word it's difficult to save it in your memory. I can work with people for weeks and still can't remember their name. You might learn the pronunciation one day, but the next day you have forgotten it. This is why reading aloud helps, as you need to hear the words. Then reading silently makes sense."

Taiwo is concerned at the lack of awareness of dyslexia in Nigeria and in most of Africa: "I would like to assist as many people as possible to get them out of the problem. Basic information is needed. Many lives would be brighter if only dyslexics could understand that they are not stupid or slow learners, but actually gifted. In recent polls, Leonardo da Vinci was voted the man of the millennium and Albert Einstein the man of the twentieth century. Both were dyslexic. This is not to say every dyslexic is a genius, but their minds work in the same manner. There are many gifts the world is losing by not recognising dyslexia. Intuition and looking into the future, for

> "In recent polls, Leonardo da Vinci was voted the man of the millennium and Albert Einstein the man of the twentieth century. Both were dyslexic."

example, are strengths that I was conscious of at a very young age. This taught me a lot about the limits of logic in reasoning and who can be said to be wise or stupid. These are strengths no school can teach and only a few people of wisdom develop in old age."

There are many ways to improve the situation: "Web-sites should be developed and accessible handbooks written to provide information. The Ministry of Education needs to be more aware and issues to do with dyslexia need to be taught about in teacher training colleges. We must limit the negative side and stress the positive side. This may then stop the exclusion of dyslexics from school and the high rate of dyslexics in prison. We need to find out why children are not concentrating at school and devise innovative teaching methods which will cater for all pupils."

SANDRA FOX

Sandra was born in Liverpool in 1960. She now works as an additional learning support lecturer in the College of North East London. Her speciality is ICT dyslexia support using assistive technologies and her expertise in this area is enhanced by her own experience of dyslexia. Sandra also works in a similar role at Wimbledon School of Art.

She found out she was dyslexic when she was 40 years old: "When I got a job as a canteen lady and also working in education, somebody said I may have traces of dyslexia. This was about 15 years ago. They said I had a slight tendency to be dyslexic: short-term memory and lack of education. There was no proper assessment. Then in 2000, I got assessed by a psychologist dealing with access to work. This was when I was working as a technician at Middlesex University and I was found to be severely dyslexic. At last I realised I could do something about my literacy problems."

> **"I didn't do any writing. I got an 'O' level in Art and went off to Art School."**

Sandra Fox

Sandra's father is from Somalia, and her mother is Irish, from County Kildare: "I was a loner as a child. I didn't play with anybody, not even my sisters. Because of my culture, I didn't go out. I just played by myself. People thought I was stupid. I didn't talk to anyone."

She ended up in a special needs school: "I had to go and see a teacher to teach me to read. The books were so basic for me at the age of 15:

Peter and Jane, Ladybird books! I never learnt to read or write. All Sandra did was go to the Art room, or play football. I didn't do any writing. I got an 'O' level in Art and went off to Art School."

Sandra describes her dyslexia: "It's like being on the outside of a secret club. What annoys me most about my dyslexia is that it's like being given a cup. It's in my hand, but the contents are trickling out. I can't control the information. Most people can go back to the full cup, but for me the cup is empty! Short-term memory is a severe problem. You either have dyslexia or you don't, but there are degrees. For some it's like a cut. You put salt in it and it hurts. Mine is like a gash, so I need to put a big bandage on it!"

This can affect your working life: "At work I was told I was stupid. I remember bringing 'The Voice' in one day and was told: 'What are you bringing that in for? You can't read!' But I could read, when I really wanted to. At that time it had poems in and I felt good about reading them."

There are particular difficulties being a mother: "When you're dyslexic, it's difficult helping your children with their homework. I used to go to my neighbours for help, as they knew about my dyslexia. Sometimes I would go to a teacher and

> **"But I could read, when I really wanted to."**

> **"It's important, particularly as a female, to assert yourself."**

sometimes I would contact a neighbour who worked for Social Services, so when you've got a question you go to the right one."

Filling in forms can also be extremely difficult: "I remember going to Social Security and was asked to fill in a form. I said, 'I can't fill it in, so can you help me?' He said, 'No, you have to go and ask a friend.' So that week I didn't get any money for my kids. I am a woman of colour, but when I can't do something because of my dyslexia, I'm treated like less than dirt. That makes me angry."

Sandra has now become more confident: "I've learnt to assert myself now. If I can't understand something, I say so. I say, 'Excuse me, explain that to me.' It used to be hard getting around, for example reading where the bus was going. At that time I wasn't ready to ask people, but now I am. If I go into a restaurant, I say, 'Excuse me, can you read that for me please?' They look at me and I say, 'I'm not stupid. I'm dyslexic.' It's important, particularly as a female, to assert yourself. I was in a pub doing some coursework and I asked this guy to spell a word for me, then another and then another! As long as you show respect to the person, they will help you."

> **"It's important to ask dyslexics if they understand something and give them the opportunity to say no."**

As a tutor, she considers the needs of dyslexic students: "It's important to ask dyslexics if they understand something and give them the opportunity to say no. Students need to have some of the information in advance, so they have plenty of time to study it. Dyslexia isn't about getting your d's and b's muddled up. It's about walking into a room and thinking, 'What am I doing here?' The education system claims it's supporting dyslexics, but when you get a nineteen-year-old coming to you, unaware of his problems, you have to think there must be something else we can try, other strategies we can adopt. Because people with dyslexia process language in a different way, they may find it difficult to follow conventional teaching methods – which is why they never learn to read and write at school."

Sandra believes dyslexics are intelligent, only in a different way. She thinks there should be more information available about dyslexia, but in an accessible form: "There should be drop-in centres, where people can talk about dyslexia, not just read about it, where you can hear things and then go out and spread the word."

MICHAEL MORAISE

Michael was born on 13 July, 1965, in Hackney, east London. He works as a qualified electrician, but has worked in many other areas, such as plumbing, driving instruction, sports and recreation. He found out he was dyslexic when he was 24 years old.

He was unemployed at the time and doing a course to get back into work: "I was writing something down and they asked me if I was dyslexic. I said, 'I don't know. I don't think so.' They said they thought it was worth me getting assessed. So I got assessed and found out I was dyslexic."

It was a revelation to Michael: "It made me understand why I had been struggling for so many years and not realising why I was struggling. I have to read things several times, for example, to take in the information. I have to concentrate on reading so that I don't stumble

> **"I was told that if I couldn't read, I would have to be a road-sweeper."**

over the words. I concentrate so hard sometimes that I miss the sense of what I have read and have to read it all again."

His short-term memory presents problems: "Sometimes I forget simple words. My short-term memory is like a sieve. I can go downstairs for something and, by the time I get there, I've forgotten what I went for and have to go back up again. That happens quite a bit."

At primary school Michael struggled to read: "My brother and sister tried to help me and they got very frustrated. All I wanted to do was go and play with my mates. I was told that if I couldn't read, I would have to be a road-sweeper. That was drummed into my head and they called me that horrible word 'dunce'."

The consequences of not being able to read could be severe: "To join the Scouts you had to read a book and I really struggled. I couldn't get in because I couldn't read it and you don't know what it is that's stopping you."

At secondary school Michael was tested and put into a special needs class: "One teacher had

> **"I used to feel such a heaviness and anxiety going places and getting lost all the time."**

Michael Moraise

to help about 20 pupils, so we didn't really get that quality of help. We were always behind and never caught up. The other classes were constantly ahead of us. I heard about algebra and wondered when we were going to do it. But that never happened because I was so behind."

Schooling ended in failure: "The shocking thing was when I did my final exam as a 16-year-old and that paper came in front of me and I didn't have a clue. I felt completely unprepared. It was like a foreign language to me. All those years studying and the results I got. I didn't get any results, to be honest. There were no results whatsoever!"

Michael's background is working-class. His parents are from Jamaica, raised in the Church of England. His mother brought up her family as a single mum, working constantly to bring in the money.

He describes how dyslexia affected him: "I find it difficult to read a map. The job I'm doing now involves a lot of driving. I used to feel such a heaviness and anxiety going places and getting

> **"Eventually, however, I managed to take my plumbing exams along with everyone else, and in order to become a driving instructor I passed all three exams."**

> **"Once we understand something, we know how to pass it on successfully."**

lost all the time. You ask someone where the place is and they tell you, but you are not taking in a word of what they are saying. 'Go left, take the second right and keep going straight on.' I just can't remember it."

But he has learnt a strategy to deal with this problem: "Now I use SatNav and I couldn't tell you when I last worried about where I was going. That works for me excellently. You put in the postcode and that's it. That stress is now completely gone. When I got the equipment, it still took a bit of time to get used to it. But the beauty of it is that it's really impossible to get lost. It will simply take you round again. If you make a mistake, it will just put you back en route, even if you get it wrong five times. And the beauty of it is that it doesn't get angry! It's the same calm voice."

This is unlike Michael's experience of some human beings: "If you're having difficulty in understanding something and the person gets frustrated, gets angry and raises their voice, then you're not taking in anything, because they're getting so angry with you. Sometimes I go into a shop and ask for a Twix and the shopkeeper says it's right there in front of me, but I just can't see it. You can tell someone you're dyslexic, but they still don't understand. They can still get really frustrated with you."

Trying to get a job can be very frustrating, even if you say you are dyslexic: "I went for a job interview as a bus controller and got no help whatsoever. I felt so humiliated when I was unsuccessful. But I also became very angry and rang up the college to find out what help I should be having. They explained that I should receive extra time and a separate room, that I could be entitled to a scribe and someone to read out the questions. Eventually, however, I managed to take my plumbing exams along with everyone else, and in order to become a driving instructor I passed all three exams. I was encouraged to learn about celebrities who are dyslexic. You don't have to be a failure and accomplish nothing."

Michael never used to read much, not even newspapers, but would watch videos and films instead. Now he realises that the more you read, the better you can manage it: "The time in my life when I got more involved in books was when I became a Christian and read the bible. I would read passages over and over again and from that time my reading has improved tremendously. When I start reading now, I can read more fluently and understand what I'm reading. But if I am making a speech, I don't have notes to read, as that just messes me up completely. I read what I have to say over and over again and learn it. Then I flow a lot better."

At home Michael and his wife have three young children and this presents problems with homework: "I really care, but I feel I'm not equipped to help them. I've had to learn a lot to help them and I've got to persevere. It's the same with the washing machine. I struggled for a long time learning how to use it. All the knobs and figures were so confusing that I just couldn't take it in."

There are advantages to being dyslexic and he gives an example from work of lateral thinking: "There was a leak in the ceiling and they put a bucket underneath, which they then had to keep emptying. My suggestion was to put a funnel in the bucket and then pipe the water from there into the drain."

He also thinks dyslexics make good teachers: "They understand that you have to explain things in many different ways. Once we understand something, we know how to pass it on successfully."

ASHER HOYLES

Asher was born in Chapeltown, Leeds in 1966. She only found out she was dyslexic in her second year at university, at the age of 25: "I was referred for assessment by the Education Department where I was studying, at the University of East London."

The main aspects of her dyslexia are to do with the way she organises herself, how she processes information and her memory: "It plays a part in everything you do, particularly in organising your thoughts and ideas. Even though I've been to university, if I was to do a piece of writing again, it would be like anew. You don't have a sense that something is done and dusted. I don't say: 'Now I can do this and so I'll just get on with it.' I do get a sense that I've improved and things don't take so long, but for the most part it affects me any time I want to articulate my ideas, especially in the written word."

> **"School was frustrating, isolating, and you're bullied. You know something's not right, but you don't know what it's called."**

Asher Hoyles

The undiagnosed dyslexia affected Asher as a child at home: "My mum, for example, would send me to the shop with a list of things to buy and I would probably come back with the wrong things or I wouldn't even be looking for the right things. It affected me because people became very frustrated. I got a reputation for being a bit stupid, or a bit slow."

It was the same at school: "I started off in the top class, as on the surface I sounded like a confident speaker. But it wasn't long before I was demoted and found myself eventually in a remedial class. I was always being told I could do better if I concentrated or if I worked harder, but nobody realised that getting 0 out of 10 every minute for Maths could have anything to do with dyslexia. People think you're slow and you get that reputation."

It also led to bullying and boredom: "You start to get bullied, not just by other pupils, but also by teachers. But more to the point, you're bored out of your skull, because you're sitting in the lesson and you don't understand what's going on. You know the teacher's speaking the same language as you, but you're not understanding what's happening. School was frustrating, isolating and you're bullied. You know something's not right, but you don't know what it's called. You know you've got this thing that you can't explain and it affects you at home, it affects you at school and it affects you on the street."

Asher's parents are working-class West Indian, her father a Methodist and her mother a Seventh-Day Adventist. The culture at home was that of West Indians in England: there was a strict discipline, you had to cook and clean, and you needed to be able to be quick on your feet, use your initiative, be supportive and not be always told what to do. But as Asher explains: "If you're dyslexic and you're still trying to even register what's being said, or you can't assert yourself because you're still actually processing what's being said, then as far as culture's concerned that's going to affect you. From a West Indian perspective you're not showing yourself as being assertive and looking about your business."

Her short-term memory was a particular source of frustration: "My dad got very impatient. I was always asked to go and do things which required memory: Go and get the hammer, go and get the nails, the screw-driver, this, that, a whole list of things, as instructions to go and do. Now, you're walking away and you know you've already forgotten most of them. And then obviously, culturally, you couldn't really turn round and say: 'I beg your pardon. Could you run that by me again!' You were expected to hold on to that: 'What, you deaf?' So in the end I devised my own little secret strategies. I knew that if I walked away and hovered around for long enough, somebody would repeat it all."

The frustration would grow and Asher remembers losing her temper a lot: "There was a complete build-up and that gave me a reputation for being rude. My mum used to say: 'You're too

> **"I needed to take my own time, to do things in small chunks. I wasn't fast or speedy."**

rude and always put your mouth push up when someone asks you to do anything.' But it wasn't really because I was rude or lazy. My mum used to say I was a really good cook, so in that respect I was all right. Also if I was left alone to do chores like sweeping up, I was all right. I needed to take my own time, to do things in small chunks. I wasn't fast or speedy.'

At university Asher received one-to-one support and got help from the Disablement Association to buy a computer which she used to complete her degree. She has had supportive friends who have been understanding about the dyslexia and tried to help her: "My husband also helps me a lot, to organise myself, and that's very important. My daughter helps me too, because she has a sense of humour about it. She says, 'Mummy, you do that because you're dyslexic, aren't you?' And she laughs, which is actually quite good, to add a bit of humour and not take it too seriously. I get support from colleagues at work too. We learn from each other. They support me because they know I'm dyslexic. Then they learn things from me about it, so it helps in the work."

A lot needs to be done to make sure people believe dyslexia exists and is not a myth: "Teachers need to be trained so they can support dyslexic students. We need resources, awareness raised about what is available, dyslexia assessment for everyone who needs it, and not

> "Because we're not blind or in a wheel-chair, where you can blatantly see the disability, dyslexics are seen on the surface just like everyone else."

just those who can afford it. It should be publicised more, so people can talk about it and be more open. People need to know how dyslexics learn and that it's not about being stupid. It affects all areas of life, so needs to be taken seriously."

At work it affects you because of your language processing and short-term memory: "People don't realise that if you're given more than one instruction at a time, or you have to take down telephone numbers, that's when your dyslexia will affect you. You may be asked for a lot of students' names, but even if you've been working with them regularly, you won't remember them automatically and that can make you appear stupid: 'You mean you've been working with those students all this time and you don't remember what they're called!'"

Another problem is finding your way round a building: "It takes you a lot longer. Someone may give you a map, for example, but I don't read a map. I can't understand it. So you have to devise alternative strategies to get to work and find your way around. The colour coding where I work is very important in helping me find my way, not that most people realise that the college is colour-coded!"

Dyslexia can also cause problems in relationships: "You perceive one thing and your partner perceives something else. And then you can clash and there's a build-up of frustration. You think they're just not understanding what's going on, even when you're explaining something. Because we're not blind or in a wheel-chair, where you can blatantly see the disability, dyslexics are seen on the surface just like everyone else. So you have to keep justifying yourself and going over the same things again and again. In general people find it hard to see why there are some things you find difficult. It's frustrating because of people's lack of imagination or lack of acceptance of what dyslexia means. You're always having to justify why you can't do certain things, rather than people accepting that you have strengths, but also areas where you're not so strong."

The strengths are not always stressed enough: "Dyslexia is not about being stupid. We are not stupid people. We have strengths just as we have weaknesses." With Asher, for example, it has made her more determined: "When I've

> **"It's a disgrace that so many dyslexics are diagnosed after they leave school."**

achieved something, it means more to me than maybe someone else, because it's such a challenge. There is a strength in finding ways to overcome difficulties. Through determination I have been able to build on my self-confidence. There are also some advantages in seeing things literally: it sheds a different light on matters. Dyslexia makes me very sympathetic to all the others who have special needs. I have sympathy because of my own position and I think that is a strength."

Dyslexics are high on the list of school exclusions, which is why Asher thinks it is so urgent for politicians to address the issue: "So many students are missing out on their education and the opportunity to contribute to society and the economy. It should be high on the educational agenda. It's a disgrace that so many dyslexics are diagnosed **after** they leave school."

DONALD SCHLOSS

Donald was born in 1959 in Dulwich, south London, and grew up in Brixton. He did not find out he was dyslexic until he was 31 years old, when he went to a Special Needs Job Search. As he says, "I was assessed over a period of weeks and received the official diagnostic assessment. But then they didn't know what to do with me!"

This is why, with three other colleagues, he founded the Adult Dyslexia Organisation, which still exists today, with Donald as its Chief Executive: "ADO was born out of that experience. They gave me access to their admin person to do some research, partly for them and partly to get materials for me, because the stuff they had shown me was for children. I didn't want to go back to Peter and Jane books!" ADO focused on adults after this research found that only 6 out of 200 dyslexia organisations were constitutionally able to deal with adults. Donald

> **"I had to sit down at home and was told you're not leaving the house till you can learn to spell your name – Schloss."**

Donald Schloss

has now been awarded the Lambeth Award for Services to the Community.

At primary school Donald went to remedial classes and clearly had problems with spelling. At home too he was punished for not being able to spell his name: "My parents didn't understand it. They saw the ability I had, but then the reports kept coming back from school that I wasn't getting the grades. I had to sit down at home and was told you're not leaving the house till you can learn to spell your name – Schloss. It wasn't till I was about 7 or 8 that I could spell it automatically."

His parents could not understand why their son's IQ score was two years above his chronological age, yet all his reports said "could do better" or "could try harder". Donald recalls, "Teachers implied that I was a time-waster. They thought I was messing around. My parents knew I was bright. As we couldn't afford a bike, I'd make one. Our spare room looked like a bicycle shop! I was always the one who took things to pieces. When something broke, I was the one who would look at it and try to repair it. I was told I could become an architect, but my dad said, 'No, that's not a proper job. It's not a trade, like a decorator or plumber.'"

> **"I was chess champion at school but I couldn't spell chess."**

When Donald went to secondary school, he was put in the top class because they went on his IQ score rather than his reports: "That was a struggle in that year – probably the most stressful period at school, especially as the top class did a lot of reading, and a lot of reading aloud. So I developed avoidance tactics, like getting kicked out of the classroom! I was constantly told I was thick, stupid, lazy."

Spelling was a major difficulty: "I was chess champion at school, but I couldn't spell chess! Words like **because** – I'd spend umpteen hours on it, but it still wouldn't stick. When writing a letter I would have to change it all to avoid a word I couldn't spell. I was very good at technical drawing and came second in the school after only one year of training on a two-year course, but I couldn't spell the things I was drawing."

Donald's mother is from Mandeville, Jamaica. His father was also Jamaican, from Kingston. Donald was brought up in the Church of England and sees himself as Black British from a working-class background. His heroes are Nelson Mandela and Martin Luther King. He thinks race is an important factor in dyslexia, as white pupils are more likely to get assessed. He has also experienced racism at an all-white conference where attempts were made to 'freeze him out', but he came up with a successful coping strategy.

Nevertheless Donald has been very successful with ADO, despite working with a very small budget and having some initial difficulties putting the name on other dyslexic web-sites. It is the only dyslexia organisation run completely by dyslexics and it has been very effective in the areas of education, employment, ICT and day-to-day living. For example, it was the first organisation to be recommended by the DfES to advise Higher Education staff and students, and the first to produce guidelines for all job centres in the UK. It also produced the first e-learning guidelines and ran a national campaign to set up adult groups.

Donald works in a dyslexia-friendly office which uses alternative systems for organisation, except for his desk which he describes as "organised chaos", as nobody is allowed to tidy it. Dyslexics and non-dyslexics work alongside each other. Spelling is not such a problem there: "I'll just ask someone and they just spell it out. They don't say 'What do you mean, you can't spell that!' They just spell it."

But he is still frustrated by having so many ideas which he can't get down on paper in time and also by constantly having to explain himself as a dyslexic. On the positive side, however, he is very good at seeing the big picture, coming up with ideas at meetings and finding solutions that other people have not seen: "People always tell

> ## "Dyslexics themselves need to be armed with the tools of knowledge."

me what dyslexics can't do. They rarely say what they can do well because of their dyslexia. I can speak faster than most, for example. I'm verbally fluent and often used that as a defensive strategy, which was my strength at school. I'm now good at gathering information, multitasking by holding several projects in detail in my head at any one time, visualising how things happen in 3D and networking."

Forgetting people's names is a continuing problem, as is time-keeping: "Since being diagnosed as dyslexic, I've got worse at getting to places on time. I've now got an excuse!" And he still has 'good' and 'bad' days: "I make sure I don't take on certain projects on a bad day!"

This is why he thinks that dyslexics have to be careful how much they reveal about themselves: "It's difficult telling a manager that you're going to have a dyslexic day when you're finding some tasks difficult to process, even though you are likely to put in more hours, working through breaks and after work. That's why you have to be careful what you tell people. In my social life, people know what I do, but I don't tell them everything. They don't understand how a Black, working-class man with dyslexia can be recognised as influential in his field and dealing with the top 50 consultants in his field in the country."

Donald's view of the future is that much still needs to be done to change attitudes, even in the dyslexia community, as dyslexia is still seen as a white, middle-class condition: "Specialist tutors are needed in schools and much more emphasis on multi-sensory teaching, reading for pleasure and thinking about solutions. More grants are needed for equipment and more definitely needs to be done in the Further Education sector, which is the weakest at the moment. Dyslexics themselves need to be armed with the tools of knowledge."

MARCIA BRISSETT-BAILEY

Marcia was born on 30 June 1973 in North London, but grew up in Hackney, East London. She now works as a Careers Adviser at NewVIc Sixth Form College in the London borough of Newham.

Her dyslexia was not diagnosed until she was 16 or 17 years old, but her mother was aware of her difficulties from when she was at primary school and she demanded support for her daughter. Marcia believes she may have been assessed by an educational psychologist, when she was asked to undertake various tasks such as putting jigsaw pieces together.

She feels the outcome may have been put down to personal and behavioural problems: "I saw someone once a week, who I now believe to

> **"We had to go round the class reading out aloud. I believe that's when I started to stammer and peers would call me a stutterer, which developed a real fear of reading, especially out aloud."**

be a psychotherapist, due to the type of activities she undertook, such as playing with a doll's house and talking to me about things which were important to me, like friends and family. My parents would come to the sessions once a month to discuss my development, as well as family life."

She remembers being very shy at school: "I couldn't read very well, so I would keep very quiet at reading time. I would like to read books which felt very safe, but were well below my reading age, like 'Peter and Jane'. I so much wanted to read, because I wanted to be normal. But words didn't seem to be a natural process for me. 'The Cat in the Hat' was a favourite, as it was the first book I could read from front to back. I remember feeling confident and good about myself."

At secondary school the difficulties continued: "We had to go round the class reading out aloud. I believe that's when I started to stammer and peers would call me a stutterer, which developed a real fear of reading, especially out aloud."

Throughout the whole experience, the saving grace for Marcia was her family. She describes her background as working class and her culture as

> **"It was a fantastic discovery that there was a name to it and that I wasn't stupid."**

Marcia Brissett-Bailey

African Caribbean. Her parents were very
supportive, even with their very limited knowledge
of the educational system, having both come from
Jamaica as young children. So too were her
grandparents. Her granddad taught her about
African history and the great civilisations of the

> **"Five years ago my mother discovered that she too is dyslexic. She always knew she had difficulties, but she wanted the best for me and was so determined for me to succeed, as she wanted me to have what she never had."**

past, which made Marcia feel very proud of who she was. She felt she had an identity and history. Her grandma's message was to work as hard as you can and be the best that you can, in whatever you do: "My mother always supported me and wanted the best for me. She helped me believe in myself and so I became very determined. She made me feel I was very important and loved."

It was when she went to Kingsway College that Marcia was eventually assessed as dyslexic and statemented: "It was a fantastic discovery that there was a name to it and that I wasn't stupid. I learnt strategies and mechanisms to get through the written world of words, for instance the word psychology, how to break it up into bits and use colours for different parts of words. I started reading more and extended my vocabulary. I would manually put the words into my memory bank. With all the support and skills learnt while at college, I was able to obtain a grade B in my GCSE for English Literature."

She describes one of the main effects of dyslexia: "It can cause confusion, so that hours just seem to disappear and one really has no idea how or where the time went. I never have difficulty in thinking what to say or having ideas as to what I want to write. I have difficulties in knowing how to spell what I want to write and this can be very frustrating. One is always being told to look words up in the dictionary, but it is very hard to look up a word you do not know visually and cannot spell."

Marcia is becoming more aware of the different aspects of dyslexia, so when she went to university, she was able to investigate the dyslexia support before she started her course: "I still had to fight for what I needed, but I knew what services were available and what I was entitled to. I also had the opportunity to be a mentor for other dyslexic students and go out and do talks about it. All this was possible because I had the emotional support of my family. In the end I did my dissertation on dyslexia, for which I received a first."

She recognises that many parents of dyslexic children still do not have the knowledge about it and are still fighting for support: "They need to know their children's rights within the education system, such as getting statemented, extra support at school, as well as the possibility of having a computer/laptop at home."

There are certain advantages Marcia sees in dyslexia: 'I think dyslexics are highly skilled because of the way they think, making any company colourful with their creative ideas, given the opportunity and support."

There is still a lot to do to raise awareness: "I think dyslexia week should be more publicised. Schools and colleges should provide clear information in their prospectuses about the support available. Some students are told they are dyslexic, but are not statemented for various reasons, one of which is cost, and this can lead to insufficient support."

Finally another tribute to her mother: "Five years ago my mother discovered that she too is dyslexic. She always knew she had difficulties, but she wanted the best for me and was so determined for me to succeed, as she wanted me to have what she never had."

BENJAMIN ZEPHANIAH

Benjamin was born in 1958 in Coleshill, Warwickshire, and grew up in Handsworth, Birmingham. He is one of the most famous performance poets in the country. He has produced numerous books of poetry and has also written several novels. Many universities have awarded him honorary degrees and he has performed his poems all over the world.

Benjamin Zephaniah

He found out that he was dyslexic when he was 21, as he recalls: "I had written a book called 'Pen Rhythm' which was quite successful. I say I had written a book, but actually I said the poems to a girl and she wrote them down. I remember there was a television programme that came on which referred to 'Benjamin Zephaniah, Britain's new young Black writer'. And that word 'writer' – I thought, I can't write and yet they're calling me a writer now! So I thought, I've really got to go and learn how to read and write properly."

Benjamin had gone to a series of schools, but hated them all. He was finally expelled from school at the age of thirteen and never went back: "I went to this very old-fashioned Church of England school with a very matronly headmistress. The teachers would say, 'You at the back!' And if I didn't quite understand something, they'd get me to stand in the corner with my hands on my head, because they said I wasn't paying attention and wasn't listening. They told me to read something and I couldn't, so the teacher would come round and ask me what I made of it.

> **"If I didn't quite understand something, they'd get me to stand in the corner with my hands on my head, because they said I wasn't paying attention and wasn't listening."**

> **"In our house there weren't really any books, but I memorised parts of the bible from a very young age and I can rap all the books of the bible."**

"I would say, 'I don't know.'

"So they would say, 'Are you paying attention?'

"I would say, 'Yes.'

"So they would say, 'Well, have you read it?'

"And I would say, 'No.'

"So they would say, 'Go and stand in the corner!'"

He also recognises a racist element that was involved: "The teacher would say, 'You're never going to be an intellectual. You're never going to be a mathematician. But you can be a sports-person!' They thought I wasn't intelligent. The teachers themselves were victims too. For them teaching was just a question of imparting information. They were right and the students were wrong. And crowd control!"

Benjamin's background is working-class Caribbean. His mother is from Jamaica and his father from Barbados. His mother realised that he had difficulty reading and writing, and used to read the bible to him: "In our house there weren't really any books, but I memorised parts of the bible from a very young age and I can rap all the books of the bible. I'm not bad at memorising words. If I was given a list of instructions, I would remember how many points there were and then go through the number to check that I'd remembered them all. When my mother started having secrets from my father, instead of writing them down, she'd tell them to me!"

After a series of petty crimes, approved school and prison, Benjamin realised he needed to do more with his life and finally enrolled in an Adult Education Class run by the Greater London Council: "Because I loved literature, I liked the idea of reading and I got quite good at it. But then I got to the point when the teacher said I was dyslexic. It was then that I had a flashback to my school days and realised what had been happening to me. I felt relieved. It's like going to the doctor, knowing you're sick, but not knowing what it is. You need to know the name of your illness, so you can go and look it up in the library."

> **"When I read a novel, even my own novel, I begin to read other words that are not there!"**

> **"Creative people don't necessarily rely on reading and writing. A number of musicians I know are dyslexic."**

There are a number of ways in which dyslexia affects him: "The main aspect of my dyslexia is writing, finding the right words and then trying to spell them correctly. For example, I can never spell the word **believe**. I now use a spellchecker. Also when I read a novel, even my own novel, I begin to read other words that are not there! Sometimes when I sign my autograph, I sign it backwards – Zephaniah Benjamin. Someone pointed it out to me and I didn't realise I was doing it. I'm also dyslexic with figures [dyscalculia]. One strategy I use is to write in code, like text messaging. For instance I will write: '2b or not 2b, that is the ?'"

Benjamin thinks reading and writing are very strange things for human beings to do: "It's a code. Creative people don't necessarily rely on reading and writing. A number of musicians I know are dyslexic. People are more aware of dyslexia now in this country, though not in many other parts of the world. More dyslexia tutors are needed to help individuals, for, although there are common elements, each dyslexic has different needs."

BIBLIOGRAPHY

Andersen, Hans Christian (1955) **The Mermaid Man: The Autobiography of Hans Christian Andersen**, London: Arthur Barker

Bain, R. Nisbet (1895) **Hans Christian Andersen: A Biography**, London: Lawrence & Bullen

Bartlett, Diana & Moody, Sylvia (2000) **Dyslexia and the Workplace**, London: Whurr Publishers

Bennis, Phyllis (2006) **Challenging Empire: How People, Governments and the UN Defy US Power**, Northampton, Massachusetts: Olive Branch Press

Blair, Maud (2001) **Why Pick On Me? School Exclusion and Black Youth**, Stoke on Trent: Trentham Books

Boder, Elena (1973) 'Developmental Dyslexia: a Diagnostic Approach Based on Three Atypical Reading-spelling Patterns', **Developmental Medicine and Child Neurology**, Volume 15

Braithwaite, Althea & Cony, Frances (2003) **Dyslexia: Talking it Through**, Bradfield, Essex: Happy Cat Books

Christie, Agatha (1977) **An Autobiography**, Glasgow: William Collins

Cline, Tony & Reason, Rea (1993) 'Specific Learning Difficulties (Dyslexia): Equal Opportunities Issues', **British Journal of Special Education**, Volume 20, Number 1

Colley, Mary (2000) **Living with Dyspraxia**, Hitchin: Dyspraxia Foundation Adult Support Group

Commission for Racial Equality (1997) **Exclusion from School and Racial Equality: A Good Practice Guide**, London: CRE

Critchley, Macdonald (1964) **Developmental Dyslexia**, London: Heinemann

Crosbie, John S. (1977) **The Dictionary of Puns**, London: Futura

Department for Education and Skills (2004) **A Framework for Understanding Dyslexia**, Nottingham: DfES Publications

Edwards, Viv (1976) **West Indian Language: Attitudes and the School**, Derby: NAME

Einstein, Albert (1994) **Ideas and Opinions**, New York: Modern Library

Evans, James S. (1983) **An Uncommon Gift**, Philadelphia: Westminster Press

Farrell, Michael (2006) **The Effective Teacher's Guide to Dyslexia and Other Specific Learning Difficulties**, Abingdon: Routledge

Fleming, Elizabeth (1984) **Believe the Heart: Our Dyslexic Days**, San Francisco: Strawberry Hill Press

Frank, Robert (2003) **The Secret Life of the Dyslexic Child**, London: Rodale

Frisch, Victor & Shipley, Joseph T. (1939) **Auguste Rodin**, New York: Frederick A. Stokes

Fromkin, Victoria A. (ed.) (1980) **Errors in Linguistic Performance: Slips of the Tongue, Ear, Pen and Hand**, New York: Academic Press

Gates, Henry Louis, Jr. (1996) 'Belafonte's Balancing Act', **The New Yorker**, September 2

Gedo, Mary Mathews (1980) **Picasso: Art as Autobiography**, Chicago: University of Chicago Press

Gill, Gillian (1990) **Agatha Christie: The Woman and Her Mysteries**, New York: The Free Press

Goldberg, Whoopi (1993) **Alice**, London: Pavilion
– (1997) **Book**, New York: William Morrow

Goldscheider, Ludwig (1959) **Leonardo da Vinci**, London: Phaidon

Grandin, Temple (1996) **Thinking in Pictures**, New York: Vintage

Hagan, Brian (2004) **Dyslexia in the Workplace: A Guide for Unions**, London: TUC

Hale, Alison (1998) **My World is not Your World**, Ingatestone: Archimedes Press

Hampshire, Susan (1990) **Every Letter Counts**, London: Bantam Press

Harris, Margaret & Hatano, Giyoo (1999) **Learning to Read and Write: A Cross-Linguistic Perspective**, Cambridge: Cambridge University Press

Hawes, Esme (1996) **The Life and Times of Pablo Picasso**, Bristol: Parragon

Hermann, Knud (1959) **Reading Disability**, Copenhagen: Munksgaard

James, C. L. R. (1960) **Modern Politics**, Port of Spain: P. N. M. Publishing Co.

Keates, Anita (2000) **Dyslexia and Information & Communications Technology: A Guide for Parents and Teachers**, London: David Fulton

Kenny, Christine (2002) **Living and Learning with Dyslexia: The Medusa's Gaze**, Salisbury: Academic Publishing Services

Leigh, Jenny (2004) **Brian has Dyslexia**, London: Red Kite Books

Majors, Richard (ed.) (2001) **Educating Our Black Children: New Directions and Radical Approaches**, London: RoutledgeFalmer

Marshall, Abigail (2005) **The Parent's Guide to Children with Dyslexia**, Newton Abbot: David & Charles

Miles, T. R. (1983) **Dyslexia: The Pattern of Difficulties**, London: Whurr Publishers (second edition 1993)

Miles, T. R. & Varma, Ved (1995) **Dyslexia and Stress**, London: Whurr Publishers

Milne, A. A. (1928) **The House at Pooh Corner**, London: Methuen

Morgan, Janet (1984) **Agatha Christie**, Glasgow: William Collins

Morgan, Pringle (1896) 'A Case of Congenital Word Blindness', **The British Medical Journal**, Volume 2, November 7

Muter, Valerie (2003) **Early Reading Development and Dyslexia**, London: Whurr Publishers

Negroponte, Nicholas (1995) **Being Digital**, London: Hodder & Stoughton

Orton, Samuel Torrey (1937) **Reading, Writing and Speech Problems in Children**, London: Chapman & Hall

Osler, Audrey (1997) **Exclusion from School and Racial Equality**, London: Commission for Racial Equality

Osler, Audrey & Vincent, Kerry (2003) **Girls and Exclusion: Rethinking the Agenda**, London: RoutledgeFalmer

Padgett, Ian (ed.) (1999) **Visual Spatial Ability and Dyslexia**, London: Central Saint Martin's College of Art and Design

Prince, Alison (1998) **Hans Christian Andersen: The Fan Dancer**, London: Allison & Busby

Pollock, Joy & Waller, Elizabeth (1994) **Day-to-Day Dyslexia in the Classroom**, London: Routledge (second edition 2004)

Pomeroy, Eva (2000) **Experiencing Exclusion**, Stoke on Trent: Trentham Books

Rack, John (2005) **The Incidence of Hidden Disabilities in the Prison Population: Yorkshire and Humberside Research**, Egham, Surrey: The Dyslexia Institute

Rankin, Qona (2006) 'Dyslexia Art and Design', in Tresman, Susan & Cooke, Ann (eds.) **The Dyslexia Handbook 2006**, Reading: British Dyslexia Association

Reid, Gavin (2005) **Dyslexia and Inclusion**, London: David Fulton

Reid, Gavin & Fawcett, Angela J. (eds.) (2004) **Dyslexia in Context: Research, Policy and Practice**, London: Whurr Publishers

Riddick, Barbara, Wolfe, Judith & Lumsdon, David (2002) **Dyslexia: A Practical Guide for Teachers and Parents**, London: David Fulton

Sabartes, Jaime (1949) **Picasso: An Intimate Portrait**, London: W. H. Allen

Scott, Rosemary (2004) **Dyslexia and Counselling**, London: Whurr Publishers

Silverstein, Shel (2005) **Runny Babbit: A Billy Sook**, London: Marion Boyars

Simpson, Eileen (1980) **Reversals: A Personal Account of Victory over Dyslexia**, London: Victor Gollancz

Singleton, Chris (2006) 'Dyslexia and Youth Offending', in Tresman, Susan & Cooke Ann (eds.) **The Dyslexia Handbook 2006**, Reading: British Dyslexia Association

Smythe, Ian, Everatt, John & Salter, Robin (2004) **International Book of Dyslexia**, Chichester: John Wiley & Sons

Steegmuller, Francis (1984) **The Letters of Gustave Flaubert 1857-1880**, London: Faber & Faber

Stone, Emma (1999) 'Modern Slogan, Ancient Script: Impairment and Disability in the Chinese Language,' in Corker, Mairian & French, Sally (eds.) (1999) **Disability Discourse**, Buckingham: Open University Press

Summerfield, Stephen & Hinton, Ron (1993) **A Social and Educational Case-History of Dyslexia**, Loughborough: LUDOE Publications

Tipper, Ann (1996) **Plees Help**, Brigg: Desktop Publications

Tregaskis, Claire (2004) **Constructions of Disability**, London: Routledge

Turney, Bob (1997) **I'm Still Standing**, Winchester: Waterside Press

Uhry, Joanna Kellogg & Clark, Diana Brewster (2005) **Dyslexia: Theory and Practice of Instruction**, Baltimore: York Press

Vaz, A. McDonald (1996) **The Doctor He Begged to Be: The Portrait of a Dyslexic**, Pittsburgh: Dorrance

West, Thomas G. (1997) **In the Mind's Eye**, New York: Prometheus

West, Thomas G. (2004) **Thinking Like Einstein**, New York: Prometheus Books

Wiltshire, Stephen (1987) **Drawings**, London: J. M. Dent

Wright, Cecile, Weekes, Debbie & McGlaughlin, Alex (2000) **'Race', Class and Gender in Exclusion from School**, London: Falmer Press

Wright, Cecile, Standen, Penny, John, Gus, German, Gerry & Patel, Tina (2005) **School Exclusion & Transition into Adulthood in African-Caribbean Communities** York: Joseph Rowntree Foundation